Friendship

A True Story of Adventure, Goodwill, and Endurance

by

Francis Mandewah

For Sister Eleanor

Sierra Leone Memories

Francis Mandewah

5/28/16

TELEMACHUS PRESS

Cover design art director: Joan Holman

Cover Photograph by Carmelo Moschitta via Roma 79, Abit. 51207 Gioia Tauro, Reggio
Calabria, Italy

Interior photographs property of Francis Mandewah unless otherwise noted.

Published by Telemachus Press, LLC
http://www.telemachuspress.com

Visit the author website:
http://www.FrancisMandewah.com

ISBN: 978-1-942899-87-7 (eBook)
ISBN: 978-1-942899-88-4 (Paperback)

Library of Congress Control Number 2016935826

MEMOIR
RELIGION & SPIRITUALITY
AUTOBIOGRAPHY

Version 2016.03.26

10 9 8 7 6 5 4 3 2 1

This book is dedicated to my friend Thomas Frederick Johnson,
his mother Virginia Elizabeth Johnson-Scholz,
and the town of Milaca, Minnesota.

FRIENDSHIP

A True Story of Adventure, Goodwill, and Endurance

Foreword

"As I chronicled my trials and tribulations I discovered my voice in between the lines of my story, a voice that was filled with faith."

—Francis Mandewah

I HAVE KNOWN Francis Mandewah since he was 15 years old, when I first met him in Sierra Leone in 1976.

Since that time, Francis has spoken to me about his deep gratitude for the ways God has worked in his life over the years, gratitude for having somehow achieved his dream of coming to the United States to pursue his studies.

However, I was astonished at reading of all the adventures, struggles, and joys that were a part of Francis' life beginning many years ago in his small village of Punduru located on the boundary between Kono and Kenema Districts of Sierra Leone.

I was enamored by his ability to share his "deep story", from relating the intimacy of relationships growing up in his village in a very remote part of Sierra Leone to the intricacies of engaging life on a reservation of First Nation peoples in the United States.

Francis' relationship with his mother affirmed for me the powerful place the African woman has in the family and the tremendous influence

i

that a mother has on her children, particularly her male descendants.

Reading Francis Mandewah's memoir was a walk back in time for me. In the early 1970s my religious congregation was invited to come to Africa to work with the education of girls. That invitation coincided with a decision at the 1972 General Chapter of the School Sisters of Notre Dame to send 10% of the Sisters to be in direct service of the poor. Over the next few years invitations were honored in five African countries: Liberia, Nigeria, Sierra Leone, Ghana, and Kenya. Some years later our Sisters from Poland opened a mission in The Gambia in West Africa.

Up until this time in Africa extended families had tried to provide for the education of their young men, but very few of the young women were afforded the possibility of secondary school learning. In 1973, four School Sisters of Notre Dame arrived in Yengema, Sierra Leone, to minister at Yengema Secondary School, opening a section of the already established school for girls.

The Sisters taught in both sections of the co-educational institute but administered the girls' school, introducing academic and practical studies that would enhance the life of the young women and thereby ultimately strengthen the life of African families. I was missioned to our community in Yengema in the fall of 1974.

Being quite young at the time, I have often quipped that those years from 1974 through 1983 provided a time of personal growth and understanding for me particularly in my "faith" life. I was, therefore, very happy to read of Francis' ability to share his relationship with God through the prayers he voiced throughout the book whether he was giving thanks or begging assistance at moments of dire need.

I had learned in my early years in Sierra Leone that Africans live their daily lives very close to God praying for protection as they lie down to sleep and without fail thanking God as they awoke from sleep. I am heartened that this tradition has remained a part of Francis' life.

To be a global citizen in today's world is to recognize in one's self the ability to welcome diversity in a non-judgmental way. The most fruitful way of achieving this skill is surely to experience diverse cultures and environments in a very personal way; feeling the blistering cold of the Sahara

Desert by night, harvesting olives and oranges from the Greek countryside, befriending the peoples of varied cultural backgrounds attempting to learn their languages so as to imbibe a new and broadened way of thinking.

Obviously, Francis Mandewah has grown in wisdom, age, and grace since I first met him as a student at Yengema Secondary School in 1976. He has used these intervening years to cultivate and maintain a deep friendship with his mentor, learning along the way of the immensity of that gift. This journey has developed in Francis an awareness of the miracles God continues to work in his life.

In opening himself to a contemplative spirit, Francis developed a sustaining prayerful relationship with his God, who provides the strength for the many questions and wonders he continues to encounter.

The continent of Africa is undergoing a great deal of change in this 21st century as I witnessed daily with my Sierra Leonean students at the University in Makeni (2008-2014). I believe it is a land of great promise! It is my prayer that one day Francis will be drawn back to his roots and play a very positive role in bringing that promise to fruition.

Sr. Rosanne Rustemeyer, SSND
Development Director
Province of Africa

Chapter 1

DREAMS ARE PECULIAR things, coming to us both when sleeping and awake. They mix imagination and memory to present images that are sometimes delightful, and other times horrific and unsettling. I have had a reoccurring dream since I was a child. In the dream, my family and I sit down to a grand feast. I walk across the room, smiling as my family applauds. At the end of the room is a small steel cage not much larger than I am. I step into the cage and the door locks behind me. A blindfold appears on my face. I begin to panic, but I hear the sound of my mother's voice, which calms me. Instinctively I feel my way along the bars to the lock. I slip a pin out of my pocket and unlock the cage. My mother and sisters rush to me and shower me with hugs and kisses.

In the dream I have passed a test and my reward is a journey. "Where are you going, my son?" I can hear my mother say. I become nervous about not having an answer for her. I go around the room frantically trying to find someone who will tell me my future. No one answers, and then the door to the room opens, flooding the room with white light. I walk towards the light and then through the door. I always awaken with the urge to know where I am going.

This dream has been the script for my life, because no matter where I am or what I'm doing, I always feel a tinge of uncertainty, as if I'm eternally looking for a flight itinerary. Through my travels, and my willingness to walk to and through the door, I discovered within myself a will to thrive, no matter the circumstance.

As children in a small village in Sierra Leone, my friends and I dreamed of travelling the world like the missionaries who opened our village school. As a British subject, I dreamed of walking the streets of London. I imagined myself in the United States visiting the places where the cowboy movies were made. No matter the destination, the key to my dreams was exiting my circumstances and stepping into a world of opportunity, the likes of which my village had never seen.

I was born just before the start of rice farming season in January 1961 in the poor but closely-knit village of Punduru, home to approximately 120 people. The phrase, "It takes a village to raise a child" was taken quite literally in Punduru. Though impoverished according to U.S. standards in the 1960s, and even more so today, Punduru was full of families who worked together to squeeze their resources in order to make do. In my youth, my village was a pristine environment where animals and humans cohabited, living in a symbiotic way.

Punduru was situated in the tropical rainforest of the eastern part of Sierra Leone in West Africa. It sat in a hilly, forested landscape, surrounded by thick bushes with trees rising high towards the clouds. The forest was alive year round, a hundred shades of green, and filled with birds and snakes and insects and so many kinds of animals. There were tall palm trees, thick bamboo cane bushes, strong mahogany trees, and a variety of plants I knew by sight. The rainy season was merciless; it was not uncommon for gusty winds to knock down palm trees along the road. During the dry season, temperatures climbed to ninety degrees, with no precipitation.

From birth to age 14, I lived with my mother, Ndoliah, and my sisters, Bettie and Amie. Our family had been larger, with five children, including me, but shortly after my birth came tragedy for our family. My father died when I was just an infant, my eldest sister Mattu died hours after being bitten by a snake in the forest, and my older brother Borboh mysteriously died in his sleep from an unknown illness. Our losses brought us closer together, and we cherished the living. My family was a constant source of love and support. As her youngest child and only living son, I knew that my mother loved and cherished me. My sisters were much older than I, so they were like second mothers to me. They would often play with me and take care of me when my mother was working, either in the field or as a midwife or herbalist.

We ate whatever we could grow, and many nights during rainy seasons my entire family went to bed hungry. Rice was the staple of our farming and our diets, but we also grew cassava, sweet potatoes, groundnuts, and cocoyam. Rice farming is seasonal, labor intensive, and dependent upon a lot of water and sunshine. The subsistence rice farmers in my village worked the land with primitive tools and were therefore never able to engage in large-scale farming.

Shortly before rice farming season began each January, farmers prepared for the season by brushing the thick bushes, felling the gigantic trees, and visiting the blacksmith. The lone blacksmith in my village made all kinds of basic farming tools by smelting either iron rods the farmers bought at market or pieces of steel removed from abandoned vehicles. Although he was slender in stature with skinny arms, he lifted the heavy hammers with little or no effort as he stretched and shaped the various tools needed by my people to cultivate the land.

Men gathered underneath the thatched roof of the blacksmith's work place, located not far from his house at the forest's edge, very early in the morning. Each man arrived with his iron rod on his shoulders. The men formed a line that eventually encircled the master blacksmith, who sat on a thick wooden bench in the middle of the men. The blacksmith's two apprentices took turns fanning the charcoal fire by pushing and pulling on a bellows made of animal skin. The other apprentice would sit next to the master and feed charcoal to the fire.

The blacksmith asked each man, "What's this for?" and the man would name the kind of tool he needed. The echoing sound from the blacksmith's heavy hammer could be heard through the forest and over the mountains.

The Punduru community remained so closely knit because of traditions like visiting the blacksmith and the activities of the village crier. Every evening while we ate dinner before bedtime, we heard the village crier's voice echoing through our forest. By order of the village chief, the town crier made important announcements to my people. This was one way we received official news, event news, or orders directly from our village chief. The crier stood in the middle of the village, cupped his two hands around his mouth, and called for people's complete attention. Everything suddenly came to a complete stop, and everybody listened attentively. After a pause, the crier began announcing the news, events, and orders. His voice could be heard clearly echoing through the forest behind my house. After a long day of rice farming, village people looked forward to hearing the news and announcements from the crier before bedtime.

I vividly remember working in the rice paddies and on the farm. In the field, the birds came early in the morning and fed on the seedlings. They'd leave during the day and return in droves at dusk. From age seven on, it was my job to drive away the pesky birds—and it was a hard job. I would wake up early in the morning, when the rice seedlings were newly planted, and head out to the field with my slingshot in hand. I would continuously yell, clap my hands, and use my slingshot to throw rocks at the birds—whatever I needed to do to drive the birds away from eating the seedlings. Sometimes my cousins and nieces would join me during my watch at the field, but mostly I remained alone as I went about my task. This very difficult job was crucial for the village's livelihood because if the birds devoured the seedlings then the crop production would fail and the harvest would be ruined.

There were other pests too. The newly sprouting rice plants drew wild bush animals out at dusk to suck the juices out of the sprouts with their sharp teeth. These pests were relentless, and made it impossible to have a very abundant harvest. Additionally, deadly Gaboon viper and cobra snakes in the forests surrounding Punduru made farming dangerous. Everyone in the fields remained on the lookout for snakes, and I was especially leery because of what had happened to my sister Mattu.

Despite the obstacles of inadequate tools, encounters with the weather, and the constant battle with birds and small predators, my people soldiered ahead and worked the land. The harvest was seldom sufficient, even though we worked so hard clearing bushes, felling trees, burning and clearing the shrubs and plowing—all done by hand with machetes, hoes and pickaxes.

I learned to harvest kola nuts at the age of six. I became proficient at climbing the various trees on my mother's small plantation, although I climbed kola nut trees much more easily and faster than cacao trees. With a kola nut tree, from standing on the ground I would grab a branch with my right hand and firmly place my left foot against the tree trunk. I would then lift myself up, springing up into the tree, grabbing a higher branch with my left hand to immediately gain my balance. Once my balance was maintained, I would continue to the very top of tree, or I would simply and freely move about in the tree by swinging from branch to branch. Climbing a cacao tree required a very different approach. I began by firmly clinging onto the tree with both hands and both feet and methodically climbed the tree by moving my entire body one hand higher followed by the other, supported by my two feet in order to reach its branches.

There was, however, one tree that I neither climbed nor attempted to harvest its fruit. In the middle of my village stood a tall orange tree with long and thick branches and plenty of leaves. For some reason, the tree attracted weaver birds. As I recall, hundreds, if not thousands, of weaver birds would flock into our village and literally take over the orange tree. Each of the birds could be seen building its nest. The sound these birds made while building their nests echoed through the forests and reverberated far beyond the earshot of my village. Interestingly, no one ever complained about the noise from the nesting weaver birds.

I remember the looks on my family's faces when I said that we were in competition with the birds for survival. The weaver birds were tipping the balance of nature against our people. The birds needed the leaves from the palm trees in the forest to build their nests. The palm tree needs those leaves to bear fruit, from which my people extracted palm oil. The leaves on the tree also made it possible for the tree to produce the naturally occurring milky alcoholic beverage—palm wine. When the birds took the leaves, the palm trees were rendered impotent and unable to produce fruits for palm oil and palm wine.

My family and I enjoyed many such conversations in the parlor of our four bedroom mud brick house. My mother often sat in the parlor and wove country cloth. My house was always filled with people. My sisters, Bettie and Amie and their husbands, each occupied a bedroom. My mother had her own bedroom, while I shared a bedroom with my sisters' children. Immediately behind our house was my mother's small plantation farm of coffee, cacao, bananas, kola nuts, cotton, pineapple, peppers and okra.

Our house was located at the edge of the forest, and the chicken coop was located at the side of the house. At one time we had more than two dozen hens, cocks, and chickens. When I was a little boy of eight, my job was to feed the chickens in the secure cage. The chicken feed was made from animal manure and rotten rice skins mixed with water. Often times, when we did not have animal manure, we had to let the chickens out into the open. This was very risky for our chickens because the mischievous hawk always sat high above the trees, ready to descend and devour our live-stock. Letting the chickens out to feed meant we could find ourselves competing with hawks over our livelihood.

Everybody in the village knew when the hawk had descended to devour one of our livestock because the chickens screamed in unison as they sought refuge from their predator. The sound of the chickens screaming reverberated through the village. This served as a notice for other chicken owners to lock up their chickens, otherwise the hawks would wind up eating all the chickens in Punduru. Many days I sat at the back of my house for hours, patiently waiting to spot the location of the hawk so I might kill it with my sling. My mother told me, "The hawk is a wise bird, hard to capture and kill." She said, "Hawks usually fly alone, because they trust no one." In my young mind, I was convinced that I could outwit my adversary the hawk and protect my family's livestock.

My poor village was composed of mud brick homes, huts, and a few cement houses with zinc roofs, situated around the large orange tree. All the houses were randomly built, scattered all about in no particular order. One house might face directly towards another house, while others faced the bushes leading into the forests. We lacked the luxury of electricity as well as running water. Drinking water was fetched from a nearby spring, which ran under some rocks half a mile away from the village. The people used other nearby streams to wash their clothes and bathe. The latrines were a few feet away from the houses, small mud brick buildings with a door, a roof, and a wall separating the men's section from the women's. Inside was a hole in the ground about ten feet deep.

The communal and festive atmosphere in my village was acutely alive year round. I recall the joyous harvest times of my early youth, celebrated with choreographed dances. Also, when the young of Punduru were initiated into either the Sande/Bondo secret society or the Poro society for boys, rites were performed in the forest. During festive season, thick white

smoke from burning firewood filled the air over Punduru as women prepared meals in clay pots squarely balanced on top of three rocks over
burning firewood.

During the girls' initiation, the village came alive with bright colored
fabric and live music. Women from other villages flocked into Punduru and
literally took over the village. Indigenous female vocalists and musicians
would sing and perform a variety of folklore songs with handmade musical
instruments. The women proudly and triumphantly danced barefoot to the
different tunes while joyously clapping their hands in appreciation of the
festive moment. During the festival, all houses in the village were open to
the singers, and the head of each household gave some token to the vocalists and their crew during visits. The energy the women needed to maintain
the jubilant and festive spirit was sustained by the abundant availability of
palm wine. Women who did not care for the alcoholic beverage maintained
their energy level by chewing on kola nuts, which provide a naturally occurring stimulant and barbiturate that induces instant and sustained energy.
The festivities continued throughout the night and ended early in the
morning when the young girls were initiated into the sacred bush.

Being born into meager conditions did not prevent me from having
special times with my mother. Since my mother was the only herbalist in
our village, and because my village lacked medical facilities, people turned
to her to diagnose and treat their ailments. My mother and I would venture
out into the forest hunting for herbal medicinal supplies. I carried a ma-
chete, a pickaxe, and a hoe. She moved swiftly, making her way along the
bushy footpath that led into the forest and then disappeared into the trees. I
had to walk fast behind her to keep up. Because I was so small my tools
were heavy and awkward, but each time I happily grabbed them and headed
to the forest with Mother. I assisted her with her harvest of several kinds of
medicinal herbs from specific tree branches, tree barks, roots, and a variety
of plant species.

Harvesting herbs in the tropical rain forest is generally a daunting task,
especially when it requires the arduous work of digging for tree roots. In spite
of the hard work, I always had sustained energy for digging simply because I
cherished being with my mother. She would point to a particular tree and I
knew exactly what to do. Using the pickaxe, I would begin digging around the

identified tree in order to first determine how deep beneath the moist tropical soil the root lay. Sometimes, after only digging a few inches I had reached my target. Other instances required me to dig further in order to reach even the first fibrous root. My mother would leave me to my digging while she went about her tasks in the forest, cautiously and tirelessly searching for specific plant leaves, or for the petals of a particular plant or shrub, while always on the lookout for snakes. I always loved digging, and I tried to do my best for my mother. On the way home from the forest, I would gather dried tree branches for firewood and walk behind my mother humming, carrying the firewood bundle home on my head.

I took pride in my mother's herbal knowledge and the medicinal wonders she performed. Once a young man I knew lay bedridden, unable to move and in severe pain. He had climbed a tree to tap it for palm wine. Although he had tied a rope around his waist and attached it to the tree, as he was tapping for palm wine at the top of the tree he slipped and fell, breaking his leg. In order to treat this man my mother said she needed special ingredients. She went to the forest alone and emerged with only leaves and tree bark. She ground the leaves and barks with snail shells in coconut oil and applied it to the young man's injury. Within two weeks after my mother's herbal application, the man was up and walking with virtually no pain.

Although English is the official language of Sierra Leone, I was raised speaking Mende, and my formal education marked the beginning of my acquisition of English. My native name was Konomueh and I was given the Christian name Francis when I began attending the village school at about age eight. My house was located within walking distance to my school. I would wake up early in the morning and wash my face and my feet before dressing in my uniform: short khaki pants and a blue shirt. My mother always made sure she gave me a few ripe bananas to eat for breakfast before I joined the other boys walking past my house to school.

There were no more than 20 students in my whole school, with fewer than five girls. All the classes were held in one room divided into five different areas, with instruction for students in grade one through grade five. We all shared one teacher, Mr. Edward Dwende.

My UMC United Methodist Church primary school began at 8AM each day with a ring of the bell. A second bell sounded at 8:30AM. Teacher Dwende waited with a cane in his hand to punish any latecomers. Each morning the students gathered and formed a perfect line for devotion, followed by marching around the windowless mud brick school building before settling into the classroom. The classroom had two blackboards, and Teacher Dwende made sure they were used wisely. We sat on a long row of benches with no desks. Each student was given pieces of chalk and a slate to write on. We learned by reciting the alphabet aloud, and we were required to bring 100 short sticks so that we could use them for counting to 100.

Shortly after the school opened, my village also got a church. Teacher Dwende was our pastor as well, and soon both children and adults in the village were converted to Christianity. Christianity was central to my elementary school education. Before I even started the United Methodist Church primary school in my village, I had already begun learning about the idea and concept of God from people in my village. On several occasions I had witnessed and observed my people invoke God, a mystical higher power, each time a terrible bad thing happened and each time something positive happened.

As a requirement of school, all students had to attend morning prayers. When it was my turn to ring the church bell for morning prayers, I slept on the floor in my mother's room the night before so that I was never late. The church bell was made from an old vehicle wheel rim hanging between two wooden posts. Using a piece of iron rod, I would strike the edge with all my might then watch as the children piled into the building.

It was through daily practice at the missionary school that I first learned to pray. We recited the Lord's Prayer and John 3:16 twice every day: once during morning prayers and again at devotion before beginning class. Looking back, I considered the words of those prayers as a key-code of sorts when trying to reach God. Church sessions were indeed boring, and in order to stay awake I would silently pray to God to make me obedient and help me remember the vital importance and connection between Christianity and education. In this way I began to establish a relationship with God as my confidant and source of strength.

After I completed elementary school, there were no tuition-free schools available at my grade level near my home. With no father or older brothers to help pay for my education, my mother arranged for me to go live with my older cousin, Alfred, his wife and their one-year-old son.

At age 14, having never been away from home before, I boarded a taxi truck headed for my cousin's one-room house in a diamond mining camp about 20 miles north of my village. The trip was over very rough and bumpy roads. I did not know my adult cousin well; in fact, we had never visited one another prior to my coming to live with him. The plan was that my cousin would assist me in getting further along in my education. My excitement over continuing my schooling overshadowed my apprehension over leaving my mother to go live with a stranger. I hoped that Alfred and his wife would be just like the other parents in Punduru and treat me like one of their own children.

The school I would attend was a United Method Church primary school in Yengema, a town much bigger than my village. During my formative years, diamond mining was big business and the headquarters of the National Diamond Mining Company (NDMC) was based in Yengema. NDMC was a huge multinational British-owned conglomerate that began operations in my country in the 1920s. In fact, in 1972 it was in this area that the third largest diamond in the world was found. It was an amazing 969.8 carats. Referred to by the diamond industry as the *Star of Sierra Leone*, it was colorless, lustrous and pellucid crystal, features that are characteristic of exceptional quality. The monetary value of such a diamond is, as one might imagine, quite astronomical. The company had a 99-year lease with the government of Sierra Leone. Under this arrangement the government received 49% of the mining profits and the company got the rest. Towards the end of the 99-year lease, when major profitable mining operations were scaled back, Kono District disintegrated into chaos, and the events that took place in that region became the storyline of the famous movie, *Blood Diamonds*. Even though I also was living in Yengema, I didn't know much about this sort of thing at the time, and it was far from my mind. All I knew right then was that I missed my mother and sisters terribly. I was homesick.

One afternoon, about three weeks after arriving from my village, I noticed my cousin Alfred looking at me with a serious expression. I tried to read his face without success. It seemed that he wanted me to say something. "I miss my mother terribly," I said to him. Alfred replied, "If you want to go back to the village, you are free to go back and live there."

Of course I wished for opportunity in my life, and because there was no opportunity for a better life in my village, my chances were better in a big town like Yengema. I began to feel that perhaps my cousin saw me as an added burden to his family, and he wished for me to leave. From that point forward, I never again let him know how terribly I missed my family in Punduru.

I came home one day and saw Alfred standing and looking in my direction as I approached the house. After greeting him and his wife, I entered the room to change my school uniform and move on to performing my evening chores. Before I could change, Alfred entered the room and grabbed me by the ears. He twisted my ears as he walked me outside to the veranda. I wondered greatly what I had done. I knew I had done all of my detailed morning chores before walking 3 miles to school. I went through the list of chores in my head: I fetched water, gathered firewood and performed all the household labor, including washing clothes and running errands. Alfred ordered me to lie down on the cement floor, and with an electric cord he had in his hand, he began whipping me mercilessly. As he whipped me, I shouted so loud that I am sure the neighbors must have heard my cries. The beating was endless, and Alfred repeated over and over, "You never disobey my wife. You belong to us. We feed you. Nobody feeds you. Go back to the village to your mother if you do not like it here."

This was my first beating in my 15 years of life. Never had I expected that I would be treated so harshly, especially by relatives. I was bruised all over from scraping my hips and elbows against the bare cement floor, and of course I endured bruises and lacerations from the electrical cord. As if the beating wasn't enough punishment and cruelty, Alfred ordered his wife not to feed me for one day. The only meal I had that day was the meal provided during school. In fact, starvation would become a frequent punishment.

After the veranda incident I wanted to know what I had done so wrong, but I dared not ever dream of asking Alfred. Much later, while at the stream washing clothes and talking with a lady I called Mama Findah, I learned that my cousin's wife had falsely accused me of disobeying her. I soon began to feel that my cousin's wife detested me living with them and would say or do anything to make me look like a bad boy to Alfred.

Whenever my cousin's wife complained about even the slightest thing, he would hit me. This continued throughout my living with Alfred, and there was nothing I could do about it. I had enough problems trying to get by in school. I was a poor student and was always struggling. Though I did my very best to keep up with my studies, it was hard since I knew nobody and received no support. Life was hard and there was never really any time to enjoy even the simplest pleasures of my adolescent years.

I began to learn more about the vital importance of diamonds in the region of Sierra Leone where I lived. Diamonds had been discovered in my country in the 1920s, and efficient mining began about a decade later. In those early days, when it rained and the topsoil washed away and the sun shone, you could see a brilliant twinkling all over the ground. Even though diamond deposits are found in many areas of my nation, the Kono District, where Yengema is located, had the highest concentration of the precious jewels. However, back in that era the local inhabitants did not know exactly what the sparkling things were, and had no idea of their value. They thought that the stars were falling down from the sky. When the country was colonized by Britain, the indigenous people were told not to touch the diamonds. In fact, they instructed them to draw a circle around the sparkling things and report their findings to the colonialists. Not realizing they were being robbed of their own highly lucrative natural resources, the people willingly complied.

The National Diamond Mining Company (NDMC) employed more than 250,000 people, with mining operations coordinated by an administrative headquarters at Yengema. People employed by the mining company were categorized as A, B, or C staffers, clerks, low level workers and finally the laborers. The hierarchy of authority was reflected in the housing facilities for each group, from the highest class to the lowest, which is where Alfred and his family and I lived.

People in the A, B and C staffs lived in bungalows which were located in the high-class residential estates in a town the size and quality of Amherst, Massachusetts. They had nice four-bedroom houses with electricity, stylish furniture, and telephones. The grass was always cut around their houses, and they had access to swimming pools. Moreover, each home had one male house servant to do the chores and to cook for the A staff family. The A staffers were also given a free vehicle with free maintenance and free gasoline. The A staff people were mostly mining and mechanical engineers, administrators, accountants, and other high level mining professionals. There were a few Africans who were mining engineers and accountants, but by far the majority of the people living in these luxurious conditions were British. Not surprisingly, the children of these privileged folks were given full scholarships for a free education. While each echelon of A and B staffs were allotted a free vehicle, there was also an NDMC-designated bus which ran on a schedule for the convenience of the staffers. It operated until midnight over well paved and maintained roads.

The highest echelons of NDMC also enjoyed several luxurious facilities. There was the Yengema Club, which had a golf course and a swimming pool and employed multiple people to keep the grass cut and maintained. There was also a golf club, a racket club, a tennis court, and even a rugby field where professional teams competed. Strangely enough there was no cricket field, despite the British influence.

The facilities also included a grocery and a supermarket where fresh meat and produce were always available. There was a fully staffed and equipped NDMC hospital with three physicians. These facilities were available only to the upper echelons. The lower classes were seen and treated by the nurses and hospital staff only. It was apartheid no doubt—subtle, yet still apartheid. There was no semblance of equality at all.

The lowest echelon of residences, where the laborers lived, was Gaia Camp. This is where I lived with Alfred and his family. The camp consisted of numerous long buildings, each with 24 overcrowded rooms. The residents of the camp lived completely separately from A, B, and C staffer bungalows. In fact, it was like an entirely different world. The conditions were extremely cramped, with two thousand families packed into the Gaia Camp living area. It was the same colonial experience that was happening all over Africa. The deprivation of the low level workers was a reflection of the greed of the colonizers and the corrupt government officials. It was a sad thing. In Gaia Camp, people had to live with hardly any privacy. There were four or five families per room. In the middle was a communal kitchen with firewood stoves that served the whole building. Running water was limited to two hours in the morning and three in the evening. There was always a long line waiting for water, and at times there was inexplicably no water.

There was a communal latrine about 20 feet away from the living quarters. This was a small cement house with a cement roof divided into two sections, one for males and one for females. Each side had five openings. A metal bucket with two handles was hung under each opening.

These were the circumstances I found myself in when I lived with my cousin. Needless to say, sanitary conditions were poor and the odors, especially in the hotter weather, were quite foul. As you might imagine, the hygiene situation was far below optimal, and the potential for severe epidemics to break out was high.

Nonetheless, I did my best to try to be content with my lot in life during those trying times. I passed the Selective Entrance Exam and graduated to secondary school, but unfortunately, Alfred abruptly stopped paying my tuition after the first year. My mother found a school in another town, Jaiama Nimikoro, about 16 miles away. She and my sisters worked together to raise the money for my tuition, room and board. Attending the school in Jaiama Nimikoro meant I had to move to that town, which came as a relief because I would no longer be living with my cruel cousin.

I moved into the school boarding house, but the conditions there weren't much of an improvement. The food was inadequate, only two meals a day: a piece of bread and weak coffee in the morning, and in the evening perhaps a small portion of rice. Not nearly enough for a growing boy.

Eventually there was no one to pay my tuition, and I was forced to move back to Alfred's home, where I sold oranges and other fruit from a basket balanced on my head, with all of the profits going to the household.

The bright spots during my life at the time were the rare occasions I was able to go and visit my mother. Although I couldn't bring myself to tell her how badly my cousin was treating me, I always felt a relief just by being in her presence. She would say, "I miss you so much that I don't even know how to do it. What do you do with this time away from your mother?" I

would tell her every boring detail of my day: how I was an excellent sales-
man, repeatedly empting my orange basket, how I did the wash, or cleaned
the house, and she would listen as if it were all breaking news. I still remember the tune she would hum as she wove cloth, asking me, "Will we
kill a chicken tonight?" I couldn't imagine making her feel sad when she
worked so hard.

Each time I visited her she wanted to know how my cousin was treating me, but I was always evasive and dismissive of her enquiry. I knew that
deep down she suspected something was amiss with me. During one visit, I
had gone with her to our cassava farm. We chatted as I walked behind her,
underneath the shade of the gigantic trees in the forest. My mother's voice
trailed off and the mood of the forest became tense. I sensed my mother
deliberately holding her breath. For a long moment we moved in dead silence. The only sound I could hear was the distinct songs of the several different kinds of birds high above in the trees. I could instinctively sense that
mother was about to ask me how Alfred was treating me, and by now I
realized I could no longer hide the truth but had to let it out. Mama abruptly stopped walking. She turned around and faced me directly, looking
straight into my eyes as if she was examining my soul and said, "So, tell me
how Alfred is treating you." Immediately after she asked the question, she
turned around and continued walking. Though I was expecting the question
I still found myself hard hit by the idea of telling. I worked to keep up with
Mama. Finally, I broke my long silence and I began explaining to her that
Alfred beat me frequently for the slightest things, and at times he told his
wife not to give me food.

As I explained the maltreatment to my mother I kept my head down,
not maintaining eye contact with her. I was afraid to look into her face and
see sadness caused by me. Mama kept listening and slipped her hand beneath my chin, raising my head to look at her in the eyes. I apologized for
not telling her the truth when she had previously asked me about my relationship with Alfred. I could see the trouble in her eyes, and she wore the
sadness draped across her shoulders. I could sense that she shared my anger
and frustration at Alfred, but I also sensed she shared my helplessness, con-
sidering the fact that neither of us could do anything to prevent or avert my
situation if I had to continue living with Alfred.

My mother stood there, staring into my eyes for what felt like an eternity. Against my will a wide smile crept across my lips. My mother was smiling, too. She said, "Well, you have to come back to the village. We can always make ends meet here. I cannot let you continue living with him so he can beat and starve you while you sell fruit for his wife." As she spoke, I tried to imagine my life in my village. Even though I knew my family could use my help with some of the physical labor on the farm, I couldn't escape the idea that I wanted to do something more with my life. I immediately protested, telling my mother that I did not wish to return to settle in the village, because there were no opportunities for me. My mother shifted my face in her hand as if to study the left side of my face and then the right. She placed my forehead against her chest then released my face. She said, "You are old enough now to make your own choices. You may go back, but remember anytime you want to, you have a place here with me."

I turned over my options in my mind. Sell fruit and dodge beatings, hoping that one day Alfred would once again begin to pay for my schooling, or return to the village to rot away as a subsistence rice farmer or become a diamond digger on the River Sewa. I didn't like either option. In truth, I saw no way out for me, until one day I met a man who would change my life.

Chapter 2

ONE DAY IN February, 1976, when I was selling oranges near the entrance of the Yengema Club, a predominately white club at the NDMC headquarters, a very tall American man with blond hair, wearing American jeans that were not hemmed but cut, a T-shirt and flip-flops exited the club. He saw me and stopped, then turned and looked at me for a few seconds. I thought he wanted to buy my oranges. He walked a few yards away from me then stopped suddenly, looking around as if someone called his name. He turned back and began approaching the door he had just exited. He kept walking past the door towards me, and when he stopped next to me, I stood up. "Hey, buddy. How much are your oranges?" he asked. He gave me exact change for three oranges. He began to peel his oranges and stood beside me as he ate. I watched his face as he ate the juicy meat of the orange. I noticed his eyes were blue like the sky just after dawn. After a long silence he asked me why I wasn't in school.

I looked at him, searching his eyes for his intentions. Why did he care? Perhaps he wanted me to do work for him. I decided to share part of my story with him. "I dropped out of school because my mother and sisters could no longer afford to pay for my school," I said in my best English.

"That's unfortunate. I bet you're smart," the blond man said with a smile.

I sensed that the man was trying to make a connection with me. In that moment I felt perfectly relaxed with this stranger. I felt compelled to explain my whole background. He sat, listening intently, as I told the story of my first 16 years of life, leaving out only the details of my cousin's cruelty. He kept listening with great interest while I told him about my plight. Although I missed my mother, I told him I could not live with her because there was no secondary school in my small village. He held up his hand for me to stop talking, and said, "Wait for me here."

He walked quickly back into the club and I sat there anxiously awaiting his return. My mind wandered to the inside of the club. I wondered who he was talking to and what all the people inside were doing. I imagined them all with cool drinks, sitting on soft chairs. After a long while the American came out with two other people, a man and a woman. All three of them stood around me; I was engulfed by their shadows. The man who had bought my oranges introduced himself as Tom Johnson. I learned that the second man was named Mike McCallie, a helicopter pilot from Perth, Australia. The Australian was also tall, perhaps a few inches shorter than Tom, and was blond too, wearing jeans and white tennis shoes. The woman looked tanned compared to the ivory complexions of Tom and Mike. She wore a mini skirt and high heels. She had dark and rather short hair. She stood with her arms folded over her chest but leaned towards me. All three of them were in their late twenties, and they all said they wanted to hear about my life.

Mike McCallie said to me, "Speak the truth, this man wants to help you with school."

I was so astounded that I told my whole story again, eagerly this time, which made me stumble over my pronunciations of the English words. They all looked directly at me and said nothing. Mike kept interrupting me saying, "Say that again, son." When I was finished, Tom stepped forward and extended his hand for me to shake it. I hesitated because I'd only ever shaken hands with a handful of adults, and never a white man. In fact, although I often saw many white people around Gaia Camp, I had never had close contact, and even less interaction, with any of them. I tried not to shake Tom's hand too hard in my excitement. We both smiled broadly and nodded our heads as if agreeing to some unasked question. He said his name again, "Thomas Johnson," and then said, "Come down to the airport tomorrow at ten o'clock in the morning to meet me."

I immediately agreed to come to the airport next day. I knew the airport well. It was about a mile and a half away from Gaia Camp, where I lived. I had walked by there before and had watched the airplanes and helicopters taking off.

I was excited and overjoyed. Shocked. Full of wonder. I could not believe my good fortune. Could I trust this man? What if he changed his mind? What would my cousin say? All the thoughts that I suppressed when I was faced with Tom, Mike and the young woman came flooding into my mind. I had no way of describing what was happening in my 16-year-old life. When I first got the news that my cousin would no longer pay for my school, then later when I learned that my mother and sisters could no longer afford my tuition either, I'd released all hope for returning to school. I desperately wanted to continue to go to school, to not grow up to be a subsistence rice farmer trapped in the village I was born in. Being offered help to go back to school was so unexpected, so out of the ordinary, that it flooded me with all kinds of new thoughts and emotions. I daydreamed about getting a good government job, having nothing to do with the mines. Or maybe I could be a teacher in primary school. The possibilities were endless.

On my way home I walked in a haze. I was in shock over the miracle that had just happened in my life. I replayed scenes from the day in my mind as I swung my empty orange basket from side to side. I saw a few boys my age on the road to Gaia Camp. I desperately wanted to tell someone my good news. I called out hello, but none of them responded. I kept swinging my basket, and I began to whistle softly. When I got home that evening I did not tell my cousin about my experience. I began to think that this miracle was something I would need to keep to myself for the moment. That night as I settled down to sleep on my mat on the floor of my cousin's house, I lay in the dark and prayed, "Dear God, I can't take any more heartbreak. Please let this be real. What did I do to deserve such a blessing? I promise to do well in school and make You proud. Please don't let me die in my sleep tonight."

In the morning, I rose early. The absolute still and quiet in the house struck a chord of fear in me. What if Alfred woke up and stopped me from going to my meeting? No. I'm going. I did my chores as quietly as possible. I took the dirty clothes to the stream. When I first arrived at the water bank the sun was still rising and there was no one else there. I took each piece and dunked it in the water repeatedly, scrubbing the fabric against my washboard. My mind drifted to a time when I would be in school. Would there be a uniform? What will we eat? Will there be races? Chores? By the time I'd worked through my basket of wash, the sun was high, beaming down angry heat, and the water's edge was filled with people doing their wash.

I stopped and talked to Mama Findah. "Young one, you are so happy this morning. God is smiling on you. Tell me: why do you smile so? Did that mean cousin of yours feed you? What is your good news?" she asked. For an instant I felt like Mama Findah could read my mind. Though she was younger than my mother, the way she treated me reminded me of being in my mother's arms. I told her, "This is the day the Lord has made. I am rejoicing, Ma." She nodded in my direction, smiling and watching as I placed one of the wet pieces of wash on my head to protect me from the heat. As I toted the wet clothes on the mile-long walk back to the house, I felt like I had lied to Mama Findah about my good news, but I sensed it might be important for me to keep this secret, even from her, for as long as possible.

Back at the house, I hung the wash in complete silence, though I desperately wanted to hum a joyous tune. I swept the kitchen floor and tidied my cousin's sitting area and then I slipped out the back of the house to hunt for firewood. When I had piled up enough wood for the day, I set off to fetch water from the tap. I made quick work of filling the plastic drum. Normally I would drag the drum the last several feet to the back of the house, but I couldn't risk waking anyone, so I kept my arms wrapped around it tightly and leaned back as I walked to the rear of the house. I took care in setting it on the ground, but it landed with a thud and a splash of water. I stood there listening for a reaction from the house, praying that God would keep them sleeping until I could escape. Though the sun was high, the house was still pitch black and I could not see any movement. I heard someone stirring on the other side of the room and tried to remain perfectly still. When the room was quiet once again I grabbed the large harvest basket and slipped out the back, heading for the orange trees along the edge of a nearby field.

An irrepressible smile crept up my cheeks. I made a dance out of my footsteps and whistled to myself along the dusty road. I sang as I pulled oranges from the branches. At one point I'd collected all the low fruit and had to place my basket on the ground so that I could climb the tree. I climbed with such energy that I made it to the highest branch before I realized how far I'd gone. I began plucking fruit and releasing it to fall into my basket. When I could no longer see my basket, only the fruit that filled and overflowed it, I descended the tree. I lifted the basket and balanced it on my head like I'd been taught to do when I was a boy of six and made my way along the dusty road to the market area near the NDMC headquarters. I sold my oranges in a haze, half in shock at the unexpected, random nature of it all and half distracted by daydreaming about what my new school would be like.

I asked one of my customers for the time and couldn't gather my basket fast enough when he said "half past nine." I headed out for my meeting with Tom. As soon as I began walking along the dusty road to the airport I was filled with doubt. What had this man planned for me? I was concerned about the risk I was taking because I did not know him. What if it was a cruel joke? What if he asked me to do something illegal? I stopped to hide my basket in the bushes along the roadside but decided to keep it with me instead. What if Alfred found out that I didn't spend my whole day selling oranges? I had never been rebellious before, so I had no idea what to expect when I returned home. I knew I could face some dire consequences, but I could instinctively sense that this meeting with Tom might be a once in a lifetime opportunity, and there was no way that I was going to let it pass me by.

Barefoot and wearing my best pants and a shirt, I showed up at the airport. The clock on the air tower said it was just before 10:00. I walked around the perimeter of the fence, peering through the chain links. The airstrip was quite busy at that time of day. I squinted through the canary yellow rays of the sun and the silver reflections off the helicopter windshields in order to see the helicopters on the ground outside the hangar. I watched pilots boarding and exiting different ones. Several men in long jumpsuits walked back and forth between the helicopters and the hangar, making adjustments to the helicopters. I was afraid to go through security because I feared being arrested or chased away. I was confused. So, not knowing what else I should do, I continued to watch the men hard at work on the airstrip.

As I scanned the area I was surprised to learn that the airport actually had three parts. Where was I supposed to be? There was a main entrance; could Tom be waiting there? And to the right of the main entrance was the hangar building. Was he perhaps inside the hangar waiting for me? And the security area was to the left. I'd have to expose myself to security in order to find out if Tom was waiting for me there. I decided security was too risky, so I settled on watching the airstrip. There were airplanes parked on the tarmac off to the left, with the helicopters on the right. I zoomed in on the right side of the fence, entertaining my fascination with helicopters. I'd always watched them fly around the areas I'd lived, but I never dreamed of being this close to them, or of meeting someone who flew them.

Tom appeared and I felt a jolt to my stomach. I stood there with my basket of oranges on my head and tears rolling down my cheeks. Tom took long strides towards the helicopters on the tarmac and started looking outside in both directions of the chain link fence. When he spotted me he raised both hands and waved to me, motioning for me to come around and approach the security gate.

The security guard's face looked confused as I approached. "This is your guest?" he said into the telephone. "You are waving to this barefoot teenaged black boy with a basket on his head? And you have a meeting with him? Sure thing," the guard said, hanging up the phone.

"What's in the basket, boy?" he asked suspiciously.

I slowly removed the basket from my head and tilted it in his direction.

"Oh, how much?" he asked, indicating that he wanted to buy some oranges.

I was relieved. I'd felt like I was about to be detained. I took his money, thanked him and headed down the hallway.

Meeting me midway down the hall, he shook my hand as everybody watched. There were a number of baffled low level African airport workers staring at Tom and me with curiosity in their eyes. What business did this Captain have with this young black boy? I noticed that they were whispering amongst themselves, some of them pointing in my direction.

Tom took me to the pilot's lounge, which was a central meeting room where the pilots gathered to talk and do paperwork. I was surprised to see so many pilots there at this time of the morning. My arrival in the lounge created quite a stir, but Tom walked past his co-workers as if he had visitors like me every day.

He sat me on a long leather couch. I placed my basket on the floor beside me as I shivered from the cold air in the room. The people inside the pilot's lounge may have been accustomed to the extreme change in temperatures from the smoldering hot sun to the icy air conditioned chill, but for me it was culture shock as it was the first time I'd ever entered an air conditioned room. My teeth chattered and the air discovered all the wet crevices caused by sweat in my clothes. I tried to stay focused and not let the cold chase me out of the room and back out into the sun.

Tom grabbed a soft drink from the refrigerator, opened it and gave it to me. I had never had one, but I didn't want to appear rude, so I took it: C-O-L-A. The can was so cold I could barely convince my fingers to continue to grip it. In fact, the liquid was so cold that when I took my first swallow the cold and the acid attacked my throat and made me spit it out. I made a mess on the leather couch. "I'm so sorry, Mr. Johnson," I said. By this time Tom was laughing. I was embarrassed. I thought I'd done something wrong. Tom just continued to chuckle until the custodian came and cleaned the couch. Tom poured my drink into a paper cup and handed it to me saying, "Call me Tom." I was able to sip the sweet liquid and appreciate the tiny acid bubbles bursting in my nose, mouth, and throat.

Tom introduced me to the other pilots. I thought I recognized Mike McCallie from the day before. "Captain Christof Balak, from Innsbruck, Austria," Tom said. He went on and on: such and such from Ireland, and so and so from Australia. Tom even introduced me to two engineers, both from England. It was as if he wanted to show me off. I wondered what he was preparing me for. After the introductions had been made, I stood there in the awkward silence. I felt my stomach rumble, and remembered that I'd yet to eat for the day.

I was seized by the urge to scream but instead I blurted out, "I am Francis Mandewah I am from Sierra Leone." I took a couple of panting gulps of air as if I'd just arrived at the end of a long run. After a pause, the room erupted in laughter and all the men came over to shake my hand. An old man wearing overalls, named Dennis Emms, asked if I was keeping all those oranges for myself. I didn't know what to say. My instinct was to sell him as many oranges as he cared to buy, but something told me it would be inappropriate to sell my oranges during my meeting with Tom. I looked at Tom, searching his face for some opinion. He looked surprised when he caught my stare. He nodded his approval, after which I sold oranges to almost every man in the room. What luck I was having! Captain Balak looked me in the eye, smiled, and said, "You are a good lad," as he shook my hand.

I was so proud when Tom told them I was his newfound friend and that he had volunteered to help me get back into school. He did not aim to just be my benefactor; he expected my friendship as well. I thought about the prospect of Tom and I being friends. How? He was so much older than I. All the friends I'd ever had were my age. I imagined Tom telling me stories about his pilot adventures and I telling him what I was learning at school. I decided that we could indeed be friends and I was elated.

Here I was, a poor boy who had known so much hardship during my young life, and I was standing with and being introduced to all of these men in an exclusive area where no other Africans were allowed. I was being treated with dignity and respect beyond anything I'd ever experienced before. I shook hands with no fewer than 10 adult white men. I felt a power greater than myself sweep over me. I knew that only God could be making all of this happen. *Why me?* I wondered. This was supernatural, a genuine miracle. Surely God placed me on that corner at that time in the afternoon selling my oranges so that Tom and I could meet. At that very moment, surrounded by a room full of new friends, I truly felt the presence of Jesus. My life was changing. This was for real.

The engineers left to go back to work and Mike excused himself to the operations room. Tom and I sat down at the counter and watched a new man walk into the lounge, grab a soft drink, and return to one of the helicopters in the field without saying a word to anyone. I watched Captain Balak run ahead of the tall slender man who took slow, deliberate strides. Captain Balak opened the helicopter door for him and then ran over to the pilot's side of the helicopter. I said, "He must be very important." I heard a loud noise come from the radio where Tom was sitting and the helicopter's engine sprang to life. The loudest whirring sound I'd ever heard whipped outside the glass, and I saw the blades turning with increasing speed until I could no longer distinguish one blade from the rest. Tom was looking intently at Captain Balak in the helicopter through the large glass window. Captain Balak raised both thumbs, and Tom responded with the same two thumbs up gesture. The helicopter slowly lifted off and vanished into the clear blue skies over the Kono District.

"That man with Captain Balak was RC Sturgeon, the General Manager of NDMC. Balak flies Mr. Sturgeon to one of the mining plants to inspect the diamond mining operations there," Tom said.

"He certainly did not look like a miner. I didn't know that men like him dug for diamonds or inspected where diamonds are dug themselves," I said, drinking the last of my cola.

"You will learn in due time. Just know that he likes to go to the mines to see the operations first hand. It's what any good manager would do," Tom said with a smile.

"Mr. ... I mean Tom, what did you mean when you told those men I was your new friend?" I asked without looking directly at him.

"I meant that from now on we look out for each other," Tom said as he turned to face me once again.

"How will I look out for you?" I asked.

"You will do well in school and make me proud. Then I can take you all around and say, 'Here is my friend Francis who has graduated secondary school.'" He chuckled and put his hand on my shoulder as he spoke.

"Very well," I said. "We look out for each other. We are friends." It was as if saying the words out loud gave the thing life.

"Tell me about yourself, friend. I know all the stuff that has happened to you, now I want to hear about what you like," Tom said.

I told him about everything that was important to me. How I had a special relationship with my mother because I was her only living son. I told him about my work in the field where I got to climb orange trees. I told him about the cramped conditions at my cousin's house in Gaia Camp. He said, "Oh yes, I know the camp. I'd like to meet your cousin. Will he be available tomorrow?"

I sat there stupefied, and after a while Tom said, "Let's go to the Catholic School." I lifted my orange basket with both hands and placed it squarely on my head and walked out the door with Tom. He told me the name of the school was Yengema Secondary School, and it was about a fifteen-minute drive from the airfield. As we left the pilot's lounge Tom walked towards a VW Rabbit and said, "Hop in," placing my basket on the back seat.

As we drove, Tom said, "I hate driving—I much prefer flying."

I laughed and said, "You should take me to school in your helicopter so you don't have to drive." He was very easy to talk to.

With a wry smile, Tom said, "I would love to, but only authorized personnel are allowed to board NDMC helicopters." He glanced at me kindly as he spoke.

"I could work for NDMC, and you could be my pilot," I replied. We laughed nonstop.

School was in session when we arrived. Tom parked the car in front of the principal's office and told me that we were going to go inside and tell the principal that I wanted to go to school.

The principal was in his office. He was a short man the color of sand and he wore a blue shirt the color of petals on summer flowers. I tried not to stare. When the petite man saw us he stood up from his desk, though this did not increase his height very much. He greeted Tom, who introduced himself as one of the helicopter pilots at the NDMC. Tom looked at me, blinking his eyes repeatedly, imploring me to speak. I took a deep breath and looked the principal in his eyes and said, "I want to go to school." The principal called his secretary into the room. He was also a short man, stocky, and also the color of sand, with bushy black hair. He wore far too many clothes for the heat: long pants and a long sleeve blazer with the school's emblem. He asked me some questions and then told me what class I was to be enrolled in.

"What is the cost of the tuition?" Tom directed the question to both the principal and his secretary. Tom immediately paid my tuition for one full year, including books and room and board. After writing out a receipt for Tom, the principal showed me the classroom that I would join. The room was filled with black boys of all different shades and sizes.

"You should have no problem fitting in here, Francis," the principal said. By this time the entire classroom was staring at me. A whisper spread through the room and some of the boys began to laugh and point. "That's enough. Back to work," the principal barked as he closed the classroom door.

Tom thanked the principal before we left the school. "Francis," Tom said as we were getting back into the Rabbit, "it's time to dress the part."

"What part? What do you mean? These are my best pants," I said, trying not to let my panic show.

"I just mean you have to wear a uniform. Don't get upset. I'll take care of it," Tom assured me.

In those days, one school uniform cost about 5 Leones, the rough equivalent of $6.00 US. Tom gave me money for my school uniforms and drove me back to towards the camp. On the way he reminded me that he'd asked to meet my cousin tomorrow. Suddenly my bubble burst. My heart began to pound as I'd hoped to keep my cousin out of my efforts to get into school. Because he refused to pay for my school fees, I assumed he did not approve of my going to school and therefore would resist all of this. I rode in silence, dreading seeing my cousin.

I asked Tom to let me out halfway home. I slipped my basket off the back seat and back onto my head, waved goodbye to Tom, and walked the rest of the way to the house. Apparently the workers who had seen me at the airport had reported the extraordinary meeting they had witnessed, and it had spread through the camp. By the time I got home it seemed as though everyone in Gaia Camp knew what was going on with me.

A boy my age fell in step with me along the path to the compound. "What interest does a pilot have in you?" he asked. "Is it work? Is there more? I want to work, too."

I walked along silently and he finally stopped asking. People were standing alongside the street looking at me. Mama Findah came over to me and put her hands on my shoulders. She looked up to the sky and shouted thanks and praise to God. The story that made it to the camp was that I was seen with the white man, one of the pilots at the airport. This was unprecedented for a 16-year-old boy.

My cousin met me on the way home and asked me if what everyone was saying was true. I confirmed it for him, and I did not leave out any details, telling him the entire story of the initial meeting, of the introduction to the other pilots, and how Tom had taken me to the Catholic school and paid for a whole year. I also told him that Tom had given me money for uniforms and shoes. I didn't share my excitement over my first pair of shoes with my cousin. I thought it might be too much good news at once. "He wants to come over and meet you tomorrow," I said, searching his face for any type of response to what I was telling him.

When we entered the house my cousin's wife was waiting. As I lowered my basket to the table she snatched it from my hands.

"What is this? You are supposed to sell these, you idiot. Do you think we live for free? Alfred, do you see what this fool has done? Ungrateful son of a goat. Alfred, you know what he needs," she said, letting the basket fall to the floor. She rolled her eyes and let out a humph in my direction before leaving the room.

I was flooded with terror. I instantly lifted my arms to protect my face and body and turned to Alfred, crying, "I sold as many as I could. I can sell more. Please."

Alfred moved silently and unplugged the cord from the iron sitting on the low shelf as I pleaded my case. He folded the cord in two and then wrapped the ends around his right hand twice. I continued to cry and back away, pleading and crying. I thought about running out of the house, but by then Alfred was standing in front of the doorway.

The first blows from the electrical cord caught me in the mid-section, smacking against the backs of my lifted arms all the way around to my back. I caught a swing in the left knee which subsequently made both my knees buckle. As I fell to the floor Alfred grabbed me by the back of the head and forced me over a chair. He continued to hold my head down and whipped me with the electric cord on my arms, back, buttocks, and legs. I screamed and cried and tried to get away. His weight on my neck began to cut off my air. He suddenly stopped and lifted my head. I felt the electrical cord brush against my lips then all the air escaped from my lungs. He was choking me with the cord, asking me if I wanted to die, assuring me he was willing to kill me if I kept upsetting his wife and running off with white men when I was supposed to be working.

I began to black out, and when I stopped clawing at the cord and my chin dropped down to my chest, he let me go. I was in remarkable pain. The welts from the iron cord throbbed and burned.

"Clean up this mess or else I will beat you again, stupid boy."

I tried to stand, but everything hurt. I managed to crawl over to the basket, and I picked up the nine oranges one by one. I didn't have the strength to make it to my mat, so I laid down on the floor and hoped that the pain on my back would subside so I could go to sleep. Sleep came and with it dreams of happier places and times. I dreamt Tom and I went for a drive up a mountain and at the top was a helicopter, which we took on a flight around the world.

The dream filled me with hope for the future. I awoke with my spirit renewed in spite of the painful sores from Alfred's beating. I went about my usual routine: I dressed quickly, performed my chores, and went to the market. The morning went smoothly. As I walked through the compound the attention that I drew from everyone was unnerving. My life had literally changed in the blink of an eye. I saw boys my age from the compound in the market, and when I said hello each of them called out to me and waved. Once a nobody, now I was a somebody. People who never even knew I was alive now stopped to look at me and say hello. They came up to me and smiled and wondered aloud at how God had smiled on me.

I was afraid that Alfred would not take me to get my uniforms, but he said that since the man was coming to the house today we may as well be able to show him what he paid for. I felt like this whole turn of events was divine intervention, and truly a miracle. Before all this happened I was living a hard life, going to bed every night hungry. I had prayed to God for deliverance from my terrible circumstances. Now the Lord had answered my prayers. He had opened up a new door for me, giving me an incredible opportunity that just one day earlier had seemed completely out of my reach. It confirmed for me what I had been taught, and what I had always known deep in my heart: that through God, all things are possible.

Chapter 3

THAT NIGHT I dreamed that Tom asked me to go to America with him. I woke up excited. I prayed, "Good morning, heavenly Father. Thank you for letting me not die in my sleep. Thank you for this beautiful day. Thank you for my new friend, Tom. And most of all thank you for school. Please help me do well today." I got out of bed before dawn and dressed quickly. I went about my daily chores, humming as I went along, imagining what my new school would be like. How would the other boys look at me? I had decided to work hard and devote myself entirely to my school work, so in my imagination the other boys faded to the background. I imagined myself alone at meal times and alone studying in my room and alone performing my chores. The image made me a little sad, but I took a deep breath and said aloud, "Your will, God."

When I arrived at the marketplace I couldn't help noticing people staring at me. A boy I had seen around camp was standing in a group at the center of the road. They shouted insults as I passed.

I removed my basket from my head and set it on the ground. "What did I do?" I asked to no one of them in particular.

The boy from around camp stepped forward and said, "The white man is sending you to school? You think you are better than us because he picked you? You aren't so special. I bet my man Momoh here is smarter than you. He should be going to school. Not you, puny little boy."

He immediately leaned forward and pushed me so hard that I lost my balance and landed on the ground next to my basket of oranges. I banged my elbow hard on the dirt and the impact of the fall irritated the welts on my back, causing me to cry from the pain. The boy stepped forward and took a handful of oranges from my basket and began passing them out to the group. Each boy began to peel his orange and subsequently throw the peels at me as I worked my way onto my feet. I raised my arm to shield my face. I wanted to shout, "It's not my fault he didn't pick you!" but I was afraid they would attack me again. So I gathered my basket and headed to the NDMC administrative compound where I knew there would be people to buy my oranges. I cradled my injured elbow in my hand while balancing my basket on my head.

Immediately upon arriving at the gate I saw a group of NDMC affiliates walking out. My basket of oranges was gone within thirty minutes. I was elated. I decided to go back through the square in order to get home because it was the fastest way. I wanted to avoid the boys who had harassed me, so I clutched my empty basket and ran as fast as I could. I stopped at the entrance to the camp because I saw Mama Findah coming back from doing her wash at the stream.

"Hello precious one. How are you today? Still happy I see."

"Oh yes, Ma. I have a lot to be happy about. I am going to go to secondary school." I traded my empty basket for her basket of wet things, and we began to walk toward the row where our houses were.

"I am so happy for you, Francis. What a fortunate turn of events in your life. You will do well. And one day you will be a big man. Important. You'll see," she said with a smile.

Though I lacked the confidence about the future that Mama Findah had, I believed that she was wise, so if she said I would do well then I thought it must be true. Still, I had my doubts. Would this be a temporary blessing affording me only one year at school again? What if Tom became displeased with me? Would he have me thrown out of school? At that moment I felt that no one could relate to how I was feeling.

Mama Findah knew about my suffering at the hands of my cousin and his wife. I wondered if she could imagine what it was like to be given a whole new life—school, a place to live, food, and clothing to "dress the part," as Tom would say. My imprisonment at Alfred's house had gone on for so long, and my thirst for schooling had been unquenched for so long that my hope had faded. Now all the pain and suffering were about to be taken away from me. I felt set free for the first time in my life. I was living a miracle. Mama Findah reached into her shawl and pulled out a small loaf of bread. She broke it into two pieces and extended one half in my direction. I took it, thanking her, and I ate the bread ravenously. I placed Mama Findah's basket on the ground in the back of her residence and we said goodbye.

That afternoon I nervously paced the floor waiting for the meeting with Tom and Alfred. Alfred and I were to meet Tom between administrative headquarters and the Separator House. I knew the Separator House was heavily fortified with electric barbed wires and guards; this was the facility where the diamonds from the three operating plants in the district were brought for processing and packaging. The Separator House was only a stone's throw away from where I lived in the Gaia Camp. I frequently watched helicopters land on its roof.

My cousin came home and freshened up from his day in the mine. I paced the room while he ate his food. When he stood up I moved quickly to the opposite side of the room. I stood staring at the floor, waiting. I heard "Let's go," and my heart skipped a beat. The walk to the meeting place took less than 10 minutes. My cousin never looked in my direction on the walk.

I saw Tom leaning against his German car smoking a cigarette. When he saw us approaching he threw his cigarette to the ground and began to walk towards us. Alfred greeted Tom with both hands, thanking him over and over, and Tom said he was pleased and delighted to help me go back to school. I kept silent. I found it remarkable how my cousin suddenly seemed to be so proud of me and happy about the opportunity that Tom was giving me. The only time Alfred ever dealt with me was when he was punishing me; otherwise, I was invisible. Even twenty minutes prior to this meeting I had been afraid he would smack me just for being in the room, and here he was thanking Tom on my behalf. Just that morning I'd thought that I might have to run away in order to get to take advantage of Tom's offer, but here was Alfred making plans for my future with Tom.

"Walk with me," Tom said and motioned us toward the light hanging on the pole along the road by the Separator House. "Do you want one?" Tom asked, extending his pack of cigarettes to Alfred.

"No, thank you very much sir," Alfred said, shaking his head.

"Francis seems like a very good boy. He is very polite," Tom said before taking a drag on his cigarette.

"Yes, yes, he is good boy sir," Alfred said with a nod of his head.

The air was hot and the sun had just finished setting and it was getting dark. Stars were beginning to populate the sky. Tom lit another cigarette and began, "Nights like this really make me miss home. Look at that sky. Not a star out of place." Tom paused to drag his cigarette and continued, "I'd love to see where you live. I've never been inside the Gaia Camp."

Alfred invited Tom to visit the house the next afternoon. I stood there under the artificial light, listening to Tom and Alfred talk. The two nodded at each other and continued to talk about me and my future as if I were not standing there. I didn't care. The fact of the matter was that I was standing with the man who had paid for my school and the man who was giving me permission to go to school. Nothing I could say could have made things any better.

We said good night and Alfred and I headed back to the house. Again he never looked in my direction on the walk. He remained silent when we entered the house. I said good night and made my way to my mat. I didn't know what to expect. The entire situation was a bit difficult to process. I sat up on my mat waiting. I could hear muffled voices. I wondered if they were talking about me. Perhaps my cousin's wife was trying to change his mind about letting me go to school. How awful. I renewed my decision to run away if I had to. At that time I felt like death would have been better than continuing to live with Alfred. I don't know how long I sat there in the dark after the voices ceased. When I felt it was safe I laid down on my mat to sleep. I prayed, reciting Our Father and John 3:16. *God, please protect me and keep me safe so that I can go to school. Please be with me in all I do. You know my heart. Please show me your will for my life. Amen.*

I awoke to a splash of cold water on my face. "Get up stupid. You cannot sleep all day. Do you think you are too good to work because you have a white friend? Get up before I beat you myself." My cousin's wife was standing over my mat.

I scrambled to my feet. "No, Ma," I said. I quickly dressed and started my daily chores. My head was cloudy. I went back and forth between worry and glee. Doubts kept interrupting my pleasant daydreams about my future.

Alfred appeared at the rear of the house while I was hanging the wash. "Come with me," he said. I expected him to walk into the back of the house but instead he walked around it. I followed him out into the road and tried to keep pace with him. Just outside the camp a large cargo truck filled with seats and crowded with people was sitting idle. "Get in," Alfred said.

I tried to suppress my panic. My mind began to race. Where was he taking me? I had to see Tom that afternoon.

Alfred reached out and smacked the back of my head, saying, "Get on the truck, stupid."

I choked back tears and boarded the vehicle, settling into a seat on the rear of the truck next to an older woman. "Where are you going?" she asked me, almost yelling in order to be heard over the truck's engine.

"I'm not sure. I'm with my cousin," I yelled. Alfred turned and gave me a dirty look. We rode along in silence. My stomach churned, and I repeatedly had to choke back tears. Why was he doing this?

After about 30 minutes I saw a sign that said 'Town of Koidu.' When the truck came to a stop the old woman stood up and so did Alfred. He gestured for me to get up and follow him. I helped the old woman with her packages and we exited the bus together. She wished me well as I walked away with Alfred. We walked down the street and arrived at a tailor shop. I breathed a sigh of tremendous relief. Inside I had my measurements taken for a white shirt and a blue blazer. The tailor had an assortment of shoes. I had never worn real shoes before. I tried on several pairs before finding a pair that fit. They had hard shiny black soles and the upper was made of dark brown leather with thin brown strings laced up the front. I could barely contain my excitement. I thanked Alfred over and over again. "How does it look?" I asked. Alfred rolled his eyes at me and turned to the tailor, asking him to package the things so that we could go. He continued to converse with the tailor until we left the shop.

We made our way back to the taxi truck, and again I rode in the back while Alfred sat up front. When we arrived outside the camp, Alfred handed me the packages from the tailor and told me to take my oranges to market. He walked away in the direction of the mine.

That afternoon when Tom showed up the camp, his arrival caused a big commotion. Pulling into the slums of NDMC in a shiny gray German car was not something that Tom did daily, nor was the sight of a white man doing this something that the people of Gaia Camp were accustomed to. Nonetheless, Tom acted as if it was nothing out of the ordinary. People gathered around the car. "Who are you here to see, sir, sir?" a man in the crowd asked Tom.

"Francis. Do you know him?"

"Ah. Yes. Francis. But he is just a boy. If you need something done you should choose a man. Like me," the man said with a broad smile.

"Maybe next time," Tom said.

As I walked out to meet Tom I heard a group of women saying that some magician must have performed voodoo on me for a white man to like me. "It was witchcraft," one woman said. My mind began to spin. I wondered whether my mother may have performed voodoo on my behalf, but I could not recall my mother ever taking me to a voodoo man. I began to contemplate how my mother could perform witchcraft. Maybe it was one of my sisters.

My thoughts were interrupted by Tom's hand on my shoulder. "Hey, Francis. What's that look on your face? Where's Alfred?"

"Look on my face? Nothing. I'm good. I was thinking ... Mr. Johnson, do you believe in God?" I asked.

Tom said, "Francis, you can call me Tom." He smiled at me before continuing. "Sure, sure. God is the creator of the entire universe and my personal Lord and savior."

I was ecstatic. I searched my heart in that moment and decided that this miracle was the work of divine intervention. I'd never felt God's presence in my life so strongly. "Let me take you to Alfred," I said, gesturing for him to follow me to the house.

As we entered the door Tom asked if my uniform was ready. I told him about my trip to Koidu to the tailor, and how I had to try on many pairs of shoes. I sensed Tom was pleased to hear my story about shopping. Tom looked around the house with my cousin and his wife. Everyone stood the whole time during the short visit. As Tom was leaving he told me he would return on Monday to take me to school.

With all of my heart I was looking forward to my new life. The spotlight was on me and this was unique and a bit scary, but I hoped that it would all be worth it. I couldn't wait to return home to my village to tell my family. I knew my mother would be happy. I didn't want to interrupt school, so I made a plan to go home to my village after I was settled in school. I wondered what life would be like in the boarding house. Would the boys be nicer than the ones around Gaia Camp? Would my teachers like me?

I had little to pack. I wore my only good pants and my only T-shirt without holes in it. I packed my blue shirt and two white T-shirts, along with my new uniform and shoes. On Monday morning I was ready to go. Alfred did not go to work that day. He stood by, along with many others, watching my departure.

Tom pulled up right on time. He got out of the car and popped open the trunk, which I was astonished to see in the front. Tom stowed my meager belongings and I climbed into the passenger seat.

The drive to the school took about 20 minutes, and Tom asked me again about my mother. He told me he couldn't imagine what it would be like to have never met his father, because he loved his dad so much. He said his parents were his best friends, and he was glad for me that my mother and I had such a special relationship. He promised that he would help me see her soon.

When we arrived, we went straight to the principal's office. The school day had just begun and the principal said I would have to change clothes in order to join my class. The principal showed me to the dorms in the back of the school. The boarding house was situated in a wooded area about a thousand feet away from the main building. The school buildings were separated by a single lane road lined with thick bushes. There were cement benches outside the boarding hall for students to gather, study, and sit in the cool shade of the tall palm trees. The water spigot was located just to the side of the entrance.

"That tap is on from seven to eight in the morning and five to seven at night. Do you understand? You have to get your water then," the principal said, slipping his hands into his trouser pockets.

"Yes, sir. Seven to eight and five to seven. Yes, sir."

"Good. Just up this hill is a bore-hole latrine. On the other side of the latrine a clear stream runs. You can wash there."

"Yes, sir. Latrine and stream. Thank you, sir."

He showed me to my assigned dorm room, which housed seven boys. The principal showed me around my sleeping area and the common area. While I was afraid of the unknown, I was at the same time very excited by the adventure of it all. I put on my uniform while Tom waited outside. When I came out I was wearing a big smile.

"Happy?" Tom asked.

"Oh yes! God is smiling on me right now," I said in a singsong voice. Tom walked me to my classroom, then shook my hand and patted me on the back before turning to leave. All the students were watching.

My homeroom teacher's name was Mrs. Mariama Fofana. She was the wife of one of the physicians at the NDMC hospital. She was medium height with dark black hair and she spoke a nasal English in a British accent. I often strained to understand her. She managed the 20 students in her class with an iron fist. I had to study very hard. I was taking math, English, English literature, religious knowledge, geography, West Africa history and world history, and economics. Passing a final examination was required to get promoted to the next form. Never a top student, I did manage to achieve passing grades.

My Catholic school's student body was made of many cultures and nationalities from all over the world. There were other African students from various parts of Africa, there were Lebanese students from Lebanon, and a few Indian students from India. The staff was also diverse and International consisting of British, Irish, Indians, Americans, and many African teachers. My homeroom teacher during my final year at YSS was Reverend Father Sean Linskey from Ireland. The boarding home provided two meals a day. In the mornings the dining hall was stocked with bread and butter and coffee. We had no lunch. Dinner would be served around 4:00 each afternoon. Many of the other boys went into town to buy food. They shared only among their groups. Sometimes Mike McCallie's wife brought me sandwiches. The boys in my dorm room did not hesitate to interrogate me about both Tom and Mrs. McCallie. "Who are all these white people in your life? What is so special about you?" they would ask.

As a teenager I was still rather short, and I was as skinny as a French waif model. The senior boys were all bigger than me and took advantage of my small stature. One day I entered the dining hall and saw my friend Sahr Fasuluku waving his arms to get my attention. I held up a finger indicating that I wanted him to wait while I got my food. When I was carrying my tray to the table, I unexpectedly tripped over something. I landed hard and spilled my dinner of rice and cassava leaves sauce all over the floor. When I looked up and around I saw Kobe, one of my dorm mates, standing with his leg extended. He had tripped me. But why?

I swept the rice back onto the tray and gathered the leaves onto the plate. Sahr and several others started in my direction. I stood up dusting myself off. Kobe was standing with a group of boys laughing.

"Very funny," I said, picking up my tray.

Kobe's smile quickly became a snarl. He charged at me, grabbing my wrist and twisting my arm behind my back, driving me against the wall while the entire dining hall looked on. "Do you have something to say, you white man's pet?"

Ambrose, the boarding home master, noticed the commotion. "Kobe, release that boy now. What is going on here, boys?" he said, pushing the two of us apart. I took a step away from Kobe and struggled to bring my arm back into alignment. I stared at Kobe while rubbing my shoulder.

He laughed and flexed his shoulders in my direction as if he was about to charge me again. "We're just playing around, sir," Kobe said.

"Well, keep your hands to yourselves," he said, turning to me as the group of boys walked away. "Are you OK? What is your name again?"

"I am Francis Mandewah. I am in Mrs. Fofana's homeroom class."

"I remember. Francis, if you have any more trouble with that boy please let me know." He placed his hand on my back for a brief moment, nodding his head.

"Yes, sir. Thank you, sir," I said, still gripping my aching shoulder.

As Ambrose walked away, Sahr stepped forward asking if I was OK. "It's so unfair," he said. "Someone should show him what's what."

"It's over now," I said, looking in the direction of the door that Kobe and his friends walked out of.

"They aren't coming back. Come. You can have the rest of my dinner. I'm full," Sahr said with a broad smile. When I hesitated he raised one eyebrow and said, "What's wrong?"

"I was just thinking that I would have to go to bed hungry and here you are offering me your food. God is indeed good," I said as I placed my uninjured arm around Sahr's shoulders.

We sat in the dining hall talking and eating for quite some time. When there were only 30 minutes left to get water we left the dining hall and made our way to the tap. There were at least seven boys waiting in line.

"I don't think we will have a turn before Ambrose turns the water off," Sahr said.

"What should we do?"

"Wait here." Sahr walked along the side of the line until he arrived at the third boy in line. "Isaac, I will give you 5 cents to give me your place in line."

The boy stood staring stupidly for a moment before finally agreeing at a price of 5 cents. When the transaction was complete Sahr waved for me to join him at the front of the line.

"You are very resourceful," I said. "I would not have been brave enough to ask. Plus, I do not have the money to pay."

"You should join me at my uncle's home this weekend. There is always a lot of food and we can throw rocks at the stream behind his house. What do you say, Francis?"

"Sure. I would love to visit with your uncle."

We carried our water jugs to our room. None of the other boys were in, so Sahr and I made quick work of washing and getting ready for bed. We reasoned that if we were asleep when the other boys arrived then we could escape torture. That night I prayed, *God, why does suffering follow me into your blessing? Please protect me from my enemies. Thank you for my friend Sahr and thank you for Tom. Watch over Mama. In Jesus' name. Amen.*

One afternoon after school in March I made my way to the airport to visit with Tom. He had been flying that day, but by the time I arrived at the airport I saw him descending. This was a rare opportunity for me to see him flying and I watched him land. Oh! How I wished Tom could just take me along in the helicopter and fly me over Gaia Camp, but I knew the NDMC policy did not allow it. I stood there with my eyes fixed on him while he sat inside the helicopter. I noticed he reached into a briefcase and took out what appeared to be a booklet. I watched as he seemed to be writing in the book before coming out of the helicopter. He immediately recognized me standing underneath the hanger shades.

"Hello, Francis. How are you, my friend?" Tom said smiling, extending his hand for me to shake. "No oranges on your head this time. Come on in with me."

I entered the pilot's lounge with him and sat on the ladder couch.

"How's school, Francis? Do you like it?"

I nodded, but of course I wouldn't tell him about the bullying for fear that with his intervention, the bullying would only escalate and I would have to drop out of school. "Have I ever told you how good I am at selling oranges? No better customer service. I can sell a whole basket of oranges like that," I said with a snap of my fingers.

We laughed. "I have a surprise for you," he said.

I was puzzled. What else could he possibly give me? I sat there silently waiting for Tom to continue.

"Loosen up, Francis. I just wanted to give you money for the taxi truck. I think you would like to go see your mother this weekend?"

My heart burst into a million happy pieces. I was stunned and couldn't find the words to thank him. Tom laughed and said, "That excited, huh?"

My eyes began to well but I choked back the tears. I didn't want Tom to see me cry.

"How about we practice your English," Tom said.

"Great. Can we work on cities of the world again?"

That night I returned to the dorm and found all of my dorm mates awake. Kobe approached me at the door and asked where I'd been. He began to aggressively pat me down. He lifted my shirt and turned my pockets inside out. "He hasn't got anything," he said, turning to the other boys. Sahr, who was small like me, sat on his bed with his knees drawn to his chin, rocking. "I guess his white father doesn't love him so much after all.

Why doesn't he give you gifts? My father gives me gifts all the time." A chorus of laughter erupted. Sahr's eyes met mine, as if he was begging me to say something, or perhaps to remain silent, I couldn't tell.

"Kobe, the disappointed African's mother gives him gifts," another boy said pointing at Sahr.

I walked over to my bed and got under the covers with all my clothes on. I was afraid that if I undressed and removed my shoes, Kobe would find the money Tom had given me. It seemed to take an eternity for the other boys to get into bed. When the room was completely quiet and dark I prayed, *Our Father who art in Heaven … Thank you, God, for keeping me another day. Thank you for my friend Tom. Please protect me and keep me safe.*

Immediately after school on Friday I put two T-shirts in a bag and left to catch the taxi truck to my village. The drive was bumpy and took more than an hour. We stopped along the way to let passengers off and load others on. The truck carried mostly women and children. There were a handful of men, including a father accompanied by his wife and three children. There were no other teenagers. My head began to throb from listening to a wailing little girl.

When we pulled into my village I was so happy that I could have burst into song. I made my way through the center of the village and arrived at my mother's door. The house was exactly as I remembered it. I found my mother sitting on a stool in front of the house weaving.

"Hello, Yeih. I have come to visit with you."

"Is that so? Well why don't you give your Yeih a big hug. You look so happy. I don't think I've ever seen you happy like this before. Tell me, Konomueh, what has happened to you?"

I lingered in my mother's embrace for several moments. I lifted my eyes to meet hers and told her, "I am in secondary school."

"Oh! Thank you, God! Really, you are in school? How? Has Alfred come to his senses?" my mother asked.

My sisters appeared in the front of the house and exploded with cheer when they saw me. "Konomueh, what have you been doing over there?"

My mother chimed in, saying, "He is in secondary school. Do you hear that, sister? Secondary school." Mother clapped her hands and stomped one foot on the ground.

My sisters said in unison, "Tell us how. What happened?"

I couldn't stop smiling and laughing. I was so thrilled by the remarkable things that were happening in my life, and the pleasure of sharing them with my family. Impatient to know why I was so happy, my elder sister blurted out, "Have you found a diamond?"

I shook my head and shared the details of my incredible good fortune and my newfound friend. They were stunned to say the least. "A white man," my mother shouted, "he will want you to pay him back."

"No, Yeih. He is my friend and he only wants to help me." My mother searched me with her eyes for a long time. I felt as though I was standing under a spotlight.

My eldest sister said, "Yeih, Francis is a big boy. He knows what he's doing. Besides, even Alfred's own children don't want to live with him." The entire room erupted in laughter.

My mother tried to fight the urge to laugh but ultimately lost her battle. "I know you are a responsible boy, Francis. I expect you to do well."

"I will, Yeih. But I miss you so much."

"I miss you too. Just love me from wherever you are and I will feel it. God will soothe your heart when you miss me. And your love will soothe my heart when I miss you." I clung to her as tightly as I could.

This visit was a stark contrast to my last visit when I'd come home sad, when Alfred and his wife kept me in misery. Although I never told my family about his mistreatment, I know they knew I was unhappy with him. They just didn't know what my specific complaint was. Now the huge smile on my face was a permanent fixture. I spent the weekend trying to forget about the mean boys in my dorm and instead enjoy being with my mother. I helped her with chores, including searching for medicinal herbal roots and bark in the forest like we did when I was a child. I worked in the field on Saturday helping harvest rice. My sisters and I prepared the evening meal together then sat after dinner watching the children play in the small yard in front of the house. I was asked to repeat my miraculous story many times, but I never grew tired of telling it.

On Sunday my mother made me a care package with roasted yams and a small piece of chicken, along with some rice. She gave me a jar of herbal tea and said, "Drink one swallow every morning. It will help you grow and gain weight." Mother walked with me to the edge of the village where I was to board the truck back to school. My throat felt as if it would collapse. Tears welled up in my eyes and fell down my cheeks.

"Oh, Francis, my dear boy. Do not cry. This is not a sad time. I am happy for you. I am in your heart. You are never really away from me."

"I love you, Yeih," I said once more as I boarded the truck. I ran to the back seat so I could wave to my mother out the back window. We pulled away and I watched her figure fade as the truck rolled along.

Later that year, in April of 1976, I was sitting in class when the principal entered the room and said, "Francis, come with me," with a beckoning motion. I left my seat and walked into the hall with the principal. Tom and Mike were standing in the hallway. They both wore serious looks on their faces. I was surprised to see Tom because I had visited with him at the airport just three days earlier. Had I done something wrong? Was Tom displeased with me? I hadn't broken or stolen anything when I was at the airport last. What could it be?

Tom broke the silence, saying, "Francis, I am going to America today." I stared at him in complete confusion. I couldn't gather a thought and I was silent for several seconds. Tom stepped towards me and put one hand on my shoulder and cupped the other hand under my chin, bringing my eyes to meet his. He repeated, "Francis I am going back to America today."

My heart dropped. I was in shock. Why was he leaving? He'd just come into my life, and now I was going to lose my friend, my benefactor. I couldn't fight the tears.

Tom continued, "Don't cry. I will send your school fees to Sister Rosanne here at school." Tears continued to roll down my cheeks, but I managed to nod my agreement.

Tom kept reassuring me. "I'd like to explain everything, but you are too young to absorb it all. I'll explain it all later." He gave me some money and said, "Put this in your pocket. I will tell my parents about you when I get home." I stood there, dumbfounded, staring at him. He finally said, "I have to go now Francis."

I followed him to the front door and watched as he entered the passenger's side of a Land Rover and Mike McCallie climbed into the driver's seat. I'd never felt more abandoned in my life. The principal walked by and asked what happened, and after I told him he simply said, "Well then. Time to go back to class." I walked to the room wiping my eyes with the backs of my arms. The students in my class had seen Tom and Mike standing outside with me, so they all knew I'd been pulled out of class for visitors.

"Did he finally dump you?" someone yelled out as I entered the room.

"That's enough. Francis, take your seat," Mrs. Fofana said.

I couldn't control the tears. When I lifted my eyes from the desk I saw Mrs. Fofana, saying, "It's OK." That night in my bed I cried beneath the covers. I prayed, asking God why he had taken Tom away. *Please don't take this life away, God. I will do whatever you say.*

Chapter 4

IF I HADN'T had my friend Sahr during the weeks immediately following Tom's departure, I may have died of a broken heart. Sahr was a slight boy with curly hair and skin the color of bamboo. His father was black, from Sierra Leone, and his British mother was white. We kept our friendship secret for fear that Kobe, Arthur and the other bullies would begin to target Sahr, too. For the most part the bullies left Sahr alone because he had an uncle who was a level C worker at NDMC, which meant, unlike me, Sahr had someone to complain to about the bullies' behavior. Sahr and I communicated through signals when other boys were around. I quickly began to avoid the bullies, and, noticing my absence, they began to actively hunt for me between classes. Sahr was a godsend. He was frequently able to warn me that a group of boys was headed my way, giving me just enough time to slip away. Many nights we sat in our room talking while the other boys were out.

One night we planned to slip away to see his uncle after Mass on Sunday. Getting away from the group of boys without drawing attention to ourselves was going to be tricky. We planned out every detail of our escape: Sahr's uncle's home was about four miles away from the school compound and we could walk there in less than an hour. Immediately after Mass on Sunday, Sahr and I would vanish from among the boys. According to the plan, because I was the faster runner between us two, I would dash off in between the houses along the road between the church and the school. I would quickly run and hide under the trees along the road toward Sahr's uncle's house. Meanwhile, Sahr would continue walking with the group of boys, including Kobe's crew, towards the dorms. According to the plan, after several minutes of walking with the boys, Sahr would suddenly stop and pretend that he badly needed to relieve himself and take off for the bushes. Once safely covered by the bushes he would walk back and meet up with me. Sahr and I would take the path through the tall elephant grass, deliberately avoiding the dusty gravel road. Our plan worked so well it became our routine.

On our first such walk through the tall elephant grasses, I walked a step or two ahead even though Sahr was leading the way. He said, "Francis, you are very lucky. This white man is paying your school fees? Is he going to take you to America?"

"I don't know. I dream of going to America for school. I want to go to America very much. I have asked him to take me, but he says he does not have an answer for me now. He knows I very much want to go to America, but I think he wants to see if I am a good enough student. I don't know. He has not said yes or no yet. He only told me to concentrate on my studies for right now. This worries me, Sahr. I am not good in math. I know Tom is watching me. I fear he will stop paying my school fees if I do not pass my exams. I am worried about my situation, my friend. What I really wish is that I could concentrate on my studies and not have to live in constant fear of being hassled by Kobe, Arthur and their friends."

Sahr said, "I hate them very much. It is unfair. I see them bothering you all the time. I wish I were bigger than them. I would fight them for you. Yesterday, when I saw Arthur throw his cup of water in your face, it made me very angry. I think they are jealous of you because the white man pays your school fees. They know you are special, Francis," Sahr said, swinging his arms, vigorously fighting an imaginary adversary.

"I know, Sahr. I am glad that you have your uncle. I know it hurts you when you see them hurting me. But could you imagine how awful it would be if they beat both of us? I have to focus on my classes. I cannot fail. I am worried that if I do not pass my classes Tom will stop paying for school, and I will be out of luck. I would have myself to blame," I told him.

"I'm worried about failing, too. You know I am not good in math, but we can always study together. We will help each other; when you do not know a math problem and I know, I will show you. We will work together. See," he said, hopping on my back, "now walk!"

Sahr's uncle's home was located in the C Staff Quarters of the NDMC about half a mile from Gaia Camp. The C Staff houses were single story bungalow homes with two bedrooms, a small living room, a kitchen, an in-house toilet, and electricity. Each time I visited, the house always smelled like something good to eat. When we got close, we could smell the aromas from the dinner that Sahr's aunt was preparing. We laughed and began to run towards the house.

We ran into the front door and Sahr's uncle was sitting in the front of the house. "Oh! Well, good to see you all. Welcome the students! I am pleased to see you both. How is school going for you two? How is the boarding home? When does the holiday start?"

Hawah, Sahr's aunt, stepped into the doorway wiping her hands on her apron. "Food is ready. Today we have sweet potato leaf stew made with dried fish and white rice."

"Ma, this is my friend Francis. He is also in the boarding home. He is supported by a white man who is a helicopter pilot."

Sahr's uncle interrupted. "Oh yes, I heard about you, son! Are you the boy in the Gaia Camp I heard the helicopter pilot befriended and sent to school?"

"Yes I am," I admitted, not knowing if I should be ashamed or not.

"How lucky are you, son! I heard the whole story about your troubles with your cousin Alfred. I have seen Alfred around but I don't really know him that well. I heard he was treating you very badly. Are you still living with him in Gaia Camp?"

Sahr interrupted, saying, "No, Uncle. He is now in the boarding home with me, and he is my friend."

"Thank God, thank God. I heard how badly he was treating you. I am so happy for you. I am so happy for you," Sahr's uncle said, hugging me and shaking my hand repeatedly. He placed his hand on my shoulder and guided me into the kitchen, looking over his shoulder at Sahr, saying, "Make sure you all study hard."

Over dinner he told us about his work in the diamond mines as a heavy duty machine operator. His job was to dig up the gravel containing diamond deposits. He told us he had often seen helicopters land near the diamond mines where he works.

"Have you ever found a diamond, Uncle," Sahr asked with a smirk.

"No, boy. If I had found a diamond I would be rich, and if I were rich I would not be living and working at the NDMC mining camp," Uncle said with a snicker before taking a spoon full of rice into his mouth. "We work digging up the gravel that contains diamonds, but we are not allowed to touch the gravel we dig up. We are carefully watched by security."

"So finding a diamond makes you instantly rich?" I asked, not sure if I would be able to believe the answer.

"Not exactly, son," Hawah chimed in. "Perhaps if you find a really big diamond, then yes, you could be instantly rich."

I started to fantasize that Sahr and I would be walking along the road and find something sparkling in the dirt. We'd work together to free the crystal from the dirt and rock and finally hold it up to the light. "I'm going to America with my half. What are you going to do with yours?" Before Sahr could answer in my imagination, Aunty Hawah was standing beside me asking if I had gotten enough, gesturing for me to take my plate to the sink.

After dinner we sat in the living room and listened to Uncle's stories about the mines. Most of them were boring, about when he had to cut through a really thick rock, but some of them were interesting, like when the big boss came down to inspect. Uncle claimed that the man came and shook his hand right as he was sitting in his rig.

That night we stayed late. Aunty Hawah had made fig pie, and we sat in the living room eating pie with the adults until it was only two hours before lights out at the boarding house. We set out on our four-mile journey back to the dorm quite content. There were no obstacles in our way. That night I prayed, *Dear God, my heart is riddled with doubts. Thank you for blessing me and keeping me faithful, Father. Please take my fear away from me so that I can do your work. I pray in Jesus' name. Amen.*

In the weeks following Tom's departure my young world had turned upside down. Sad and lonely now, I often stood alone, with tears rolling down my cheeks. Once the principal walked by and asked me what was wrong, and I explained that I was still upset over my friend leaving the country. For him and the other boys in the school it was just an interesting and rather curious turn of events, but for me it was a huge personal loss that hit me like a bolt of lightning from a clear blue sky.

Not knowing what else to do, I struggled to walk. Making matters worse, the two boys who were in the hall when I was talking to the principal were standing in the road between the school and the boarding house, mocking me and laughing at me as I made my way to the dorm. "Where's your white hope now?" they yelled. I asked myself if my miracle could only be temporary. Out of their jealousy, these boys were happy that circumstances had taken a downward turn for me. It was an emotional roller coaster for me, and a burden too heavy to bear at that age.

I was seriously concerned that I would have to drop out of school again. In my mind I struggled with worries that after the year was over Tom would no longer send any money for my education. These thoughts and fears left me troubled and conflicted. Many nights I had trouble falling asleep. The mystery surrounding Tom's departure made matters worse. If he had told me what happened and why he had to leave the country so abruptly, then I would know that he was OK and therefore I could be OK. His promise to send the money through the School Sisters of Notre Dame meant the world to me, but I was not sure that it would actually happen. Of course I wanted to believe him, but I must admit that I'd had little experience with trusting adults completely, aside from my mother. I was always a bit suspicious of people's motives, which made me doubt Tom's promise. The emotional turmoil was awful. I'd gone from feeling on top of the world one minute to having it all come crashing down on me in the blink of an eye. I feared returning to live with my cruel cousin.

My imagination ran wild. I knew that as a pilot Tom was involved with diamond shipments. Was it possible that he stole some diamonds and was caught and told to leave? Or was it possible that I had somehow misunderstood what my friend told me? I didn't think so. I understood Tom's American English quite well, certainly better than I did his other friends, like his best friend, Dennis McFadden, who spoke with such a thick Irish brogue that I could not easily comprehend much of what he was saying. Mr. McFadden used the word *bloody* quite often, and I soon learned that it had nothing to do with actual blood. In any case, the one thing I was sadly sure of was that after only two months my friend and benefactor had left me. All I could do now was carry on until I graduated in 1979, when I'd be 18.

One day, weeks after Tom had left the country, I decided it was time for answers. I made up my mind to ask Tom's friends what happened to him. I made my way back to the airport in hopes of seeing Captain Balak and Mike McCallie. When I arrived at security the guard teased me about carrying oranges on my head. He laughed and wished out loud that I had some now. I walked past the metal detector and made my way to the pilot's lounge where the men congregated. Mr. Smallman, the engineer, was sitting on the same leather couch I had spilled my first cola on. I walked over and asked if he knew where I could find Captain Balak or Mike McCallie. He told me that they were both out flying. Mr. Smallman looked me up and down then averted his eyes out the window toward the hangar. He said flatly, "Tom Johnson is no longer here." I stood there trying to phrase a question that I could put to Mr. Smallman, but I had no luck finding the words. I left the lounge without saying goodbye and I walked from the airport to the NDMC Security Headquarters to see Dennis McFadden. I had made up my mind to ask him why Tom had to leave Sierra Leone so abruptly.

The NDMC security headquarters employed over 10,000 security personnel, who were on standby 24 hours a day, ready to spring into action to prevent and deter illicit mining and arresting illicit diamond miners found digging within the NDMC demarcated zones. Dennis McFadden was Security Chief. When he saw me coming, he shouted in a loud voice, saying "Frankie, come here." Everyone was surprised that he would call out to a young black boy. He told me to come over to his office at three the following day.

The next day he told me, "Don't worry Francis, Tom will send your school fees, OK?" He reached into his pocket and took out some money. He handed it to me saying, "Put it in your pocket, and study hard at school." As I put the bills in my pocket, I felt a sudden relief at being reassured by one of Tom's best friends that Tom was planning to keep his promise and send my school fees. But I was still curious to know why he had to leave, and I sensed that Mr. McFadden knew what I wanted to know. I shifted my weight from my right foot to my left and pushed my hands into my pocket. I found a spot on the floor and began to tap it with my toe. The silence was deafening. Whatever Mr. McFadden knew, he did not tell me, and despite whatever I might have been curious about, I did not ask him either.

On my walk back to my dorm I wondered how McFadden could have known Tom would send my school fees. Did Tom talk about me? My mind continued to come back to the prospect of stolen diamonds. Was Tom caught and therefore told he must leave the country? Although now I can think of many reasons someone might abruptly leave their job, at the time no thoughts or reasons besides diamond theft could came to my mind.

Just over a month after Tom left, I was in class one afternoon when Sister Rosanne, one of the American School Sisters of Notre Dame came into my class and asked to speak to me outside of class. She told me she had received a letter from Thomas Johnson with a check for $120 American dollars for my school fees and expenses. Sister Rosanne said, "I will hand over the check to the school principal. The money will be held in the school's account to be used as you need it."

My heart overflowed with joy. I reproached myself for doubting Tom. This experience marked the start of my ability to trust another human being. Just as Tom could have easily picked someone else to send to school, he also could have turned his back on me when he left the country. He had indeed kept his word. One night I prayed, *Thank you, God, for teaching me faith and trust. Thank you for placing Tom in my life. Thank you for keeping and protecting me from death.*

About one month after Tom sent my school fees, Sister Rosanne reappeared at my classroom. This time she handed me a letter from Tom. I was elated to hear from my friend personally. I ran down the hall and out the back door quickly. I made my way to sit under the palm trees behind the school building. I opened the letter and began to read my friend's words to me:

Dear Francis,

What a journey I've been on. I can't wait to tell you all about it. I told Mom and Dad about you. The flight from Sierra Leone

went through London then home to Minnesota. I hope everything is going well. Study hard and I will continue to send your
school fees to Sister Rosanne. God bless.

Your friend,
Tom

I read his first letter over and over, hoping to find his explanation for
why he had to leave Sierra Leone that abruptly. I searched all his subse-
quent letters for clues, too. Although I never found any answers, I began to
save all his letters, along with the letters that began arriving from Tom's
mother, Mrs. Virginia Johnson.

I clearly recall the first package I received from Tom's mother in
America. When the boarding home master appeared at my dorm room
door, I was relieved that only Sahr and I were in. I immediately opened the
package and I closely examined its contents in absolute admiration: one pair
of American blue jeans, two pairs of cotton underwear, two white T-shirts
and two pairs of socks. Sahr stood by as I immediately tried everything on,
and we were amazed that every item I tried on fit me perfectly. I thought
about how Tom would've had to describe me for his mother to guess my
size so precisely. The package truly boosted my morale and began our relationship. In her generosity, kindness, and caring, I felt an emotional connection to her. Her letters and affection filled a hole in my heart where my
own mother could not stand. Just like Tom, she too must have felt for me
living in dire poverty.

"Put those things away before Kobe and the others come back," Sahr
said, pacing the floor with his hands resting on top of his head. As I put the
clothing away in my trunk, I found a sealed white envelope underneath the
two white T-shirts. When I finished stowing my items I crawled into my
bed to open the envelope. I found a letter, pictures of Mr. and Mrs.
Johnson, and $10 in US currency. Sahr sat at the foot of my bed, watching
as I read. The letter said:

Dear Francis,

How happy I am that God has brought you into our life. Tom tells me that you are a very good boy. I hope these things fit. I will be talking to you a lot in the coming days.

We Love You,
Virginia Johnson

I read the letter aloud to Sahr and I showed him the $10 bill that was folded into the letter. I had never seen American money. I examined it carefully, taking notice of the detail inscription on the bill.

"Wow, what will you do with the money?" Sahr asked.

"I will go to see my mother in the village," I said with a smile. Since my country used a different currency, I would change the money at a bank in Koidu.

"Good. You must never let Kobe and the others see your new things or your money. They will take them just so that you cannot have them," Sahr said with a serious look on his face.

He was right to warn me. It seemed that everybody in the dorms and at school soon found out that I had received new clothes from my white friend in America. The bigger boys took turns pushing me and insulting me. I became hesitant to wear my T-shirts and jeans for fear of more envy and bullying.

A month later I received another letter from Tom, from Yukon Territory, Canada. The letter contained three photographs: one photo of him dressed in thick winter clothing and two photos of mountains covered with white snow. He wrote that it was currently too cold in Northern Canada. The pictures were so vivid that I could feel the chill. I had never seen photographs of snow. I'd seen pictures of snow in books that I read in school, but these photos were almost real. It seemed as if I could reach out and touch the icy cold surface. I thought snow mostly came from America and England. The pictures made me feel like I was having a new experience, and they made me feel closer to Tom. His letter said he had just taken a new job flying for Mayo Helicopters in Vancouver in Canada's province of British Columbia and in Hawaii. Clearly, he was moving on with his life in new and exciting ways. I began to wonder if we would ever spend time together like we used to after school at the airport.

Chapter 5

WITH TOM GONE, I felt isolated and lonely both at school and in the boarding home. I had left my cruel cousin only to fall into a similar situation at the dorms. I reported it to the principal a few times but my complaint was always dismissed as "boys play."

About one month before I graduated from high school in 1979, I received a letter from Tom, sent from the city of Abidjan in West Africa.

Dear Francis,

I have arrived in Africa. I am on the way to Upper Volta in Bobo-Dioulasso where I will be stationed. I would like you to come to Bobo-Dioulasso.

I was very happy to receive this good news. I was excited, but I kept my excitement to myself for fear that if the boys found out I would be bullied even more, and possibly even seriously harmed, which could prevent me from pursuing my dream.

Wanting to know why Tom had to leave Sierra Leone wasn't my only curiosity. We never had gotten to know each other that well, so I had a long list of questions. By now, despite wanting answers to some questions, I fully trusted Tom. He had always kept his word to me. This was another turning point in my young life, and I was determined to confront and endure the challenges.

One afternoon Sister Rosanne handed me a telegram from Tom. "Ticket arranged to Bobo-Dioulasso via Abidjan. Pick up ticket at Air Afrique office in Freetown." I was so elated over the good news that Tom would be living in West Africa and wanted to see me that I almost panicked.

The good news indeed marked another turning point in my life. I would leave my home, my family and my country, and possibly not return home for a long time. I had no idea if I would be gone for days or years, but I felt very happy about my new adventure. This would be my first ride in an airplane and my first time travelling outside of the area surrounding my village. In my heart I knew this was a step forward and the beginning of a new opportunity for me.

Even during my excitement I was apprehensive and conflicted; my thoughts and emotions were mixed equally with glee and anxiety. First, I continued to be thankful to God that Tom had continued to care about me and was now giving me the opportunity to travel outside my country. I quickly realized that the opportunity presented an immediate challenge: in my country, to get a passport one has to know someone in the government. I was a poor boy from a small village who did not personally know any government officials in Freetown.

I racked my brain for ideas on how to obtain a passport. The idea of going to Freetown alone for the very first time frightened me terribly, but I was determined to face the challenge. I was learning that opportunity comes with risks and challenges; much later in my adult life I fully came to grasp the reality that life will always present risks, challenges and opportunities. At 19, I was determined to face the challenge. I was desperately in need of someone with political connections in Freetown.

Luckily, I had a schoolmate whose father was a political figure in Freetown, one who I hoped might help me obtain a passport, but I was reluctant and hesitant to tell anyone that Tom had sent me an airline ticket and that I would soon leave the country. Initially I kept the good news to myself because I feared the bully boys would escalate their violence against me and attempt to physically harm me to prevent me from leaving the country.

After much contemplation I reluctantly approached the schoolmate whose father was a politician and told him I needed his father's help to obtain a passport. I told him I knew no one in Freetown who could help me get a passport. My schoolmate looked at me wide-eyed and blurted out, "Are you going to America?" I immediately assured my schoolmate that I was not going to America. I feared telling the truth at the moment while still at school. My schoolmate told me he was sure his father would help me obtain a passport, and he would accompany me to see his father in Freetown.

Away from the school compound, on the way to Freetown, I finally revealed the truth about my travel plans to my schoolmate. I explained my reasons for not telling the truth while I was still at school. He indicated that he was aware of the jealousy, bullying and envy I was subjected to at school by the other boys simply because I was sponsored by a white man. Once we began talking openly, my schoolmate became even more curious to know more about my travel plans. I told him frankly that I wished I was going to the United States, but that I was going to another West African nation, Upper Volta. I invited him to come with me to the airline office where I would be issued the ticket.

In Freetown my schoolmate introduced me to his father and mother and I explained my situation fully. My schoolmate's father assured me that he would be able to help me obtain my passport without difficulty. With my travel plans set, I sent Tom a telegram saying, "Passport obtained expect me within a few days."

I returned back to Punduru to say goodbye to my mother, sisters and my village. I knew it was going to be an emotional parting. When I arrived, several of my sisters' children were outside playing hide and seek in the banana bushes behind our mud brick house. The children told me that my sisters and their husbands and adult children were at the rice farm. It was harvest time in my village and festivities had just begun. I was happiest to visit my family in my village during harvest time. My mother was in the parlor weaving country cloth when I walked in. When I first laid eyes on her I began to fully realize that I was leaving my family and my village and it could take me a long time to return home. I waited until my sisters came home from the farm in the evening, and after we all had supper. I told the entire family at once that Tom now wanted me to visit him in another country in Africa, and probably live with him for a while. I told them with tear-filled eyes that I was leaving the country, and I would not see them, perhaps for many years. My brother-in-law blurted out, "You going to the white man country?" The rest of my family remained dead silent with all eyes fixated on me.

I explained, "No, I am not going to the white man's country, but I am leaving our own country and going to another country within Africa." I showed my family my new passport and I said that I had come to say goodbye to them before returning to Freetown in a few days from where I would depart. It was quite an emotional moment when I said goodbye to my mother and sisters.

When I left Punduru, as it happened I would be virtually cut off from my family for 10 years, with no contact of any kind. In 1979, my country lacked telephone service. Post offices were virtually unheard of in villages like mine. The only functioning telephone service in the country at the time was a government operated telephone exchange service in Freetown, 205 miles away from my village. I thought about my nieces and how they would be growing over the years. I understood that by leaving I would miss out on life with my family. The opportunities that waited for me did little to soothe the heartache.

With my small suitcase in my hand, I arrived at the Lungi International Airport in Freetown early in the morning, though my flight was not until the afternoon. I stood and watched people arriving and leaving in buses and in cars, police officers directing traffic, and every hour I saw one of the huge airplanes taking off and another approaching the airport from afar. I checked in early at the Air Afrique counter, and as I waited at the lounge for my flight I marveled at the sight of the huge airplanes on the tarmac. I wondered how such a large and heavy machine could rise up from the ground and take off with so many people inside it. While I was excited to be making my first flight, I was acutely afraid that the airplane might just fall out the sky, which would end of my life and ensure that I would never meet my friend, and would be a loss to my mother and family.

The flight to Bobo-Dioulasso took about four hours with a stop-over in the city of Abidjan. As I took my seat, I methodically examined the inside of the airplane. I noticed that the air hostesses were all females who spoke in English when asked, but I heard them speaking mostly in French. I sat by the window next to a man I thought was Lebanese. The air inside was very cold for me. As the plane taxied out onto the runway, I watched with great eagerness as one of the air hostesses demonstrated by holding a device in her hand and putting it over her ears and mouth. I did not understand what the demonstration was all about. Soon I heard the powerful engines roaring and the plane began running at a high speed. I began to see Freetown far below as I felt a funny sensation. Soon I noticed we were all leaning back as if we were climbing a hill. I began to see clouds below and soon I noticed we were no longer climbing a hill. The temperature inside was cold. People began to get up from their seats and walk. The man sitting next to me lit up a cigarette and soon I noticed several people smoking.

During the flight I had a million thoughts. My emotions were mixed and my mind kept wandering to apprehensions and anticipations. While I felt very fortunate to be leaving the country and I knew Tom was giving me an opportunity, I was at the same time conflicted and full of apprehensions. Even though I had met with him repeatedly during the first two months we were acquainted, I still knew little about his life, and he knew little about mine. I had mentioned in several of my letters to him that I wished to go to the United States for school, but in his last letter he said he wanted to get to know me more before he could decide whether to continue to sponsor me. I thought this was fair, and I was prepared to be tested.

My anxiety over living with him had a lot to do with the fact that I had never had my own room and had only ever lived with family or in the boarding house with other boys. Tom's bungalow residence at NDMC, which I never visited, was from a whole different world compared to my mother's mud brick house. Now I suspected I would be living with him in the same household, and this frightened me. I feared doing something stupid, or behaving in a mischievous fashion, appearing a rascal, which might discourage Tom from further sponsoring me. I was very much aware that going to America, and for school in particular, involved a lot of money. I doubted if Tom was willing to undertake such a responsibility.

I tried to still my mind with thoughts of what the house would look like, where I would sleep that night, and life with Tom on a daily basis. For a time, dreams of hot baths, a clean bed, and maybe a pool out back soothed my racing mind.

The flight touched down at Bobo-Dioulasso airfield in the late after-noon. On the far right of the airfield I saw several helicopters and small airplanes parked outside and several white men working inside the hangar. With my small bag under my arm, I walked towards the hangar where the helicopters were parked. A short man with dark hair began walking towards me. He met me halfway and said, "Are you Francis?" When I said yes, he extended his hand for me to shake and waved me to walk along with him to the hangar. He told me Tom was expecting me and was currently flying, but would soon be landing in about 30 minutes.

As I patiently sat and waited for Tom to land, I watched helicopters taking off and landing. I watched as helicopters came into view, lower and lower until I could see them clearly. I instinctively kept my eyes fixated on the helicopter that Tom was piloting as it descended to the earth and landed. He sat inside the aircraft and took some time to do his paperwork. I was so happy in that moment. I stood at attention waiting for Tom to emerge. I was wearing long khaki pants and the same shoes Tom had bought me three years earlier.

Tom shook my hand when we greeted. I could tell he was delighted to see me after so much time. He told me he had returned to Africa with his girlfriend, Shauana, and that she was at the house with their baby daughter, Tarashaun. It had been a long time since I last saw my friend, so I was shy and reserved, and I sensed Tom noticed my timidity and shyness. At the house Tom introduced me to Shauana. My first impression was that she seemed nice.

The modern three-bedroom house was everything I expected. The house was located in a fenced compound where only the pilots and engi-neers lived. I was the only exception. The compound had an old African watchman who camped outside the compound's gate at night under a makeshift tent. I spent significant time chatting with him and I sensed the old man, who spoke French, was quite content with his job. I also sensed he had wondered about my special relationship with the white family. Although no Africans were allowed in the compound, the old man saw that I was absorbed into the midst of the white family.

I could not believe that God was making all this to happen to me. I was at first very shy and reserved in the house; I confined myself mostly to my bedroom and came out only when it was time to eat. About two weeks after I arrived, Tom and I had a conversation after dinner. He told me he was delighted he had met me in Sierra Leone, and was happy he helped me back to school. He said he knew my goal was to ultimately go to the United States for school, and said, "Let's see what happens, Francis. For now, you stay with us here. You stay with us and work for us taking care of baby Tara." I was eager to ask him why he had left Sierra Leone, but I felt it would have been disrespectful to ask the question, especially in that moment.

I got along fairly well at first with Shauana. I was respectful and obedient to her at all times. I did most of the household chores, even though we also had an old African lady who assisted with most of the chores and with the baby. We enjoyed a peaceful household for a time. Soon I also came to know all the pilots and engineers of Viking Helicopters at the Bobo-Dioulasso base. These men worked at the Viking Helicopters bases in Tamale, in the West African nations of Ghana, Lama Kara, Togo, and Bouake in the Ivory Coast.

Since French was the official language in Bobo-Dioulasso, I wanted to learn the language. I made friends with a young French man named Mousa who worked at the Centre Les Scouts de Haute Volta (The Scouts of Upper Volta), a government operated public program for youth, and I visited him there often. The Center provided free activities and lodging, and many French travelers from France were guests of the center. I enrolled in a basic conversational French class at the center and soon noticed several others became interested in me because they wished to practice their English with me. I was reluctant to hold conversations in English because I needed to learn French, so in the end I made a deal with my French friends. I agreed to hold conversations with them on alternating days in English and French. Soon I could hold basic and fluent conversations in French.

At the center I met a friend named Rudi Kretschmer who had traveled to West Africa from Bochum, Germany on a motor bike, a Yamaha XL 500, through the Sahara Desert. Rudi was very friendly and we immediately became friends. I listened to him in disbelief as he described his trek through the world's deadliest desert. I thought riding a motorbike across the Sahara was craziest thing anyone could do. Little did I know that Rudi's trek would soon inspire me to embark on my own perilous trek through that desert. Our friendship, made in 1979, was quite a memorable one, and it continued for many years thereafter.

In late 1980, Tom was transferred to the West African nation of Ghana to be chief pilot in Tamale, so we relocated to that city. When I first heard about the move I was excited because I thought it meant I would finally get to fly in a helicopter with Tom. Much to my dismay, Tom was only allowed to transport his immediate family in the company-owned helicopter, so I had to take the two-day dusty road route to our new home. The Viking base in Tamale was close to two of the major rivers where the WHO was working to eradicate tsetse fly infestation and the disease of river blindness.

In Tamale we lived in another modern home compound where only white people lived. The home had four bedrooms and a swimming pool. The compound also had a night watchman and each home was assigned a male Africa servant who did all the household chores, including cooking. I noticed our male servant did not seem to like me that much. He once admitted to me that he disliked me simply because I was black. I soon came to know most of Tom's friends, including an Italian engineer named Stefano who was in Tamale on an Italian government construction project. Stefano's wife and Shauana clicked and soon became friends.

By mid-1981, relations between Shauana and I became difficult and we were not getting along. She claimed I was spoiled and that I didn't know the value of a dollar. She demanded I leave the house. One night after dinner Tom said, "Francis, it's time for you to go. You have to leave the house. I want you to stand on your own feet for two years. After that, I may consider sponsoring you to go to the US for school." I had no reason to doubt Tom's promise. He had not let me down in the past and I had no reason to believe he would let me down this time around.

I must admit that I was angry about having to move out of the house because by that time I had gotten used to the upper class lifestyle: the good and nutritious European foods, and a clean, private bedroom in the same house as Tom, Shauana and baby Tara. But I realized I had to prove myself to Tom. I had to show him that I was worthy of his generous, altruistic support. I had to set myself a goal that was meaningful and worthwhile, and I had to fervently work towards that goal and achieve it at all costs.

Not wishing me to endure hardships in a foreign country, Tom had secretly secured a job for me with his friends at a British construction project north of Tamale. The crew was constructing a bridge over the White Volta River north of Tamale in a town called Bawku. Tom had arranged for me to be employed at the construction project as a mechanical store keeper. I thanked him and told him that I did not wish to work for the project. When Tom heard my plan to go through the Sahara Desert to Italy to work for Stefano's family, he looked me straight in the eyes for a few good seconds with an unblinking frown. I am sure he was wondering if I was out of my mind to turn down a job he had helped secure for me. When Tom realized how serious I was, he said, "Do you realize how dangerous it is in the Sahara? Don't you understand that it's a no-man's land?" I sat quietly at the dinner table listening to Tom with baby Tarashaun on my lap while Shauana was busy in the kitchen. Finally, Tom said, "Well, I will talk to Stefano." I felt a huge relief. Tom spoke to Stefano, and luckily Stefano said that he would write his relatives in Italy and tell them about me wanting to come to Italy to work for them at the hotel.

My proposed adventure came with challenges and complications. First, I needed a visa for Italy and I obviously needed money for the entire trip. Because Tom had already given me his blessing, I hoped he would give me some money to cover the travel expenses. My assumption turned out to be right when Tom gave me $300 in US currency. Since I had never handled such a significant amount of foreign currency before, Tom advised me to immediately purchase US travelers checks with half the money, and change the rest into French francs, which was the currency used in the French speaking West African countries of Ivory Coast, Upper Volta, Senegal, Togo, Benin, and Mali. I wrote Rudi a letter and told him my idea of traveling through the desert to Italy and asked for his financial assistance. Rudi was extremely generous and sent me $400 US. With $700 under my belt, I felt more confident to embark on my journey through the Sahara.

With my tourist visa for Italy in hand, I felt prepared, but in spite of the bravado confidence I displayed to Tom and myself, deep down I was afraid and hesitant. What would crossing the Sahara prove? What if I did not get along with Stefano's family? I reminded myself of Tom's promise to revisit the topic of school in America after two years of living on my own. I had a zeal for adventure, but the most exciting thing I had done was climb cacao and kola nut trees—so to me, this was a rite of passage. I wanted to be able to survive and cope in unknown territory.

In preparation, I purchased $400 in US traveler's checks. I took a blanket from the house and two pairs of pants, two shirts and a handbag. I secured the traveler's checks in the waistband of my khaki trousers, a trick I had learned back at the boarding home to protect my currency from thieves. With sufficient local currency in my purse, along with my passport, it was time to venture out into the unknown world.

Chapter 6

BEFORE I COULD go through the Sahara Desert, I had to get there. In Tamale I boarded an overcrowded truck destined for Bamako, the capital city of the West African nation of Mali. The passengers were a mixture of women with their children, and older men. I was surprised to hear many different languages; I had expected to converse in French. The truck's engine was loud, and thick black smoke came from the exhaust. Several children were crying in their mother's arms even while some were being breastfed.

I tried to still my mind by reflecting on the history and physical geography of West Africa I'd learned about in school. I wondered, as we drove along, if this was the land of the empires of Old Ghana, Mali and Songhai, all of which had once been rich and powerful empires. I imagined that I was seeing the historic significance of the country of Mali and the historical sites of Timbuktu and Gao unfold before me just outside the truck window. One of my best subjects in school was West African History, and I thoroughly enjoyed the stories of the King Mansa Musa, who was the richest king in the world at one point in history. I could envision what the region looked like as merchants caravanned across the desert to trade in gold and salt. I loved the details of the caravan trade across the Sahara by Arab traders of North Africa. I dreamed of visiting the ancient city of Timbuktu to visit the UNESCO designated historical site where the Manuscripts of Civilization are housed.

I was jarred out of my thoughts by a woman tapping me on the shoulder. She extended an orange to me, and as I took it I noticed her little girl sitting quietly eating an orange, smiling with a dirty face. I remember thinking how lovely it was to be a child in a mother's care. I thought of my own mother, who always gave me fruit to eat. I thanked the woman in French, though I am certain she did not understand me, and I settled back into my daydream as I looked out the window again. I remembered the Arab traders from North Africa who traded slaves taken from among the Sub-Saharan African peoples, and I had to work to get back to my more pleasant thoughts about the history and geography of the landscape I was passing through. I realized that studying the history and geography of a particular place is one thing, but being physically present, inside the environment itself, and knowing its history is quite another experience.

The truck ride was long and dusty. I don't think I had ever traveled over so many potholes in my life. After six hours in a cramped truck, we arrived and the driver let us out at the marketplace in central Bamako. The city was like most Western African cities with a large Muslim population; the men dressed mostly in long, bright, colorful gowns and they wore hats. I was delighted to use the little bit of French I had learned from my friends in Bobo-Dioulasso. I was able to engage in conversations with people as I walked around at the huge open air marketplace. Hungry and exhausted from the hours of riding in the truck, I stopped by a female vendor at the marketplace and bought white rice with peanut gravy and meat. I noticed the woman staring at me as I ate hurriedly so I wouldn't miss the transport truck to my next destination: Segou.

As I sat at the central marketplace waiting for the next transport to depart, I noticed scores of Malian women wearing big, attractive golden earrings. Their ears had numerous piercings and in each piercing hung a large golden earring. These women also had dyed their lips black.

The ride from Bamako to Segou took only a few hours and it was mostly over semi-paved road with bumpy potholes. The truck galloped on its way, seeming as if it would tilt over in one direction. When I finally got off the truck in Segou, I looked out and gazed at the mighty River Niger, one of the longest rivers in West Africa. I found a transport truck driver who spoke French and could help me catch a ride in an over-crowded truck that was just about depart to my next destination, the city of Mopti. The truck was peopled by women and toddlers, with just a few men on board. It seemed to me that most of these women were traders who had come down to the city to purchase. In addition to holding on to at least one child, each woman gripped either a stack of packages or a large shopping bag. I assumed they were returning home.

I suspected the women onboard spoke mostly in their local dialects, so I was leery about trying to start a conversation. I sat silently among them and became uncomfortable when the women began to stare at me. I turned to the old man in the seat next to me and attempted to hold a conversation in French. He had a white beard and wore a white hat. The moment I uttered my first word in French, all the women became very quiet and even more of them began staring at me. The old man only gave me a strange, chilling look. I wondered if he spoke French but was not willing to hold a conversation with me. Or perhaps he did not speak French and therefore could not respond to me. I spent the rest of the trip in awkward silence.

We finally arrived in Mopti very late at night, and my fellow passengers quickly vanished into the dark. They obviously had reached their final destination. The French-speaking driver told me that the next transport to Gao would be the following morning. It was now pitch black and I stood there in the dark trying to decide what to do. The marketplace/transportation depot was dark and dead silent. I could hear goats and sheep bleating at the moon. I found an empty trading bench and sat down as the driver pulled off into the darkness, taking with him the brightness of his headlights.

With nowhere to go, I sat down on the wooden table with my bag next to me, contemplating my next move. The reality was that I had to wait until morning, which did not arrive as soon as I hoped. I laid down on the bench with my bag underneath my head and fell into a deep sleep until I was awakened with a jolt by the mosque's loudspeaker announcing the morning prayers. I sprang up and saw people arriving at the marketplace on foot, by bicycle, and on mopeds. The place was quickly becoming crowded.

I bought a breakfast of a mug of coffee diluted with condensed milk and a loaf of buttered bread and boarded the transport truck to Gao. This truck, too, was overloaded with women and children. As I traveled further north, I noticed the men were dressed like Arabs, wearing long robes and head wraps. I was relieved to find myself beside a French-speaking old man. He stroked his long white beard and asked me, "What are you doing here? Where are you going?" I told him I was going to Algeria, which was the next country on my itinerary. He looked at me with concern on his face and said, "The Sahara Desert is dangerous. Be careful." Of course I knew I was taking a risk by going through the Sahara. Tom had tried to impress upon me just how dangerous my trip would be. I understood the risks, and I was a little annoyed by the old man's warning.

The overcrowded truck stopped in several small villages. At each stop there were women and young children selling food items along the road-side. I noticed one young girl carrying a large basket of oranges balanced on her head without any support from her hands. She reminded me of my younger self, and each village made me think of Punduru. Were the roads being paved back home? Could my sisters and nieces be among the women and children selling goods to travelers? I called out in French to the young girl with the oranges. "How old are you?" She did not answer but she responded by showing me her oranges. I took four and deliberately gave her a larger bill. As she was trying to make change, I walked away, waving my hands for her to keep the change. She stood there looking at me as I boarded the transport truck destined for Gao. Whatever the little girl thought, I will never know.

On this leg of my journey, we crossed the River Niger. It originates in the historical region referred to as the Funta Jallon highland of Mali, near Timbuktu and Gao, and it flows through several countries in West Africa and finally empties itself in the Atlantic Ocean. This was another moment where I realized the difference between experiencing the history and the wonder of the world and studying them in classes. I noticed the vegetation changing as we traveled through the countries along the west coast of Africa towards the Sahara Desert in North Africa. The vegetation along the west coast was mostly tropical, with tall trees, huge branches, and leaves forming a canopy of foliage; rainfall was plentiful, so the soil was moist. But moving northwards from Mopti towards Gao, I began to notice grassland, with very few short trees and much more sand in sight.

I finally arrived in the city of Gao late in the afternoon. I conversed in French with a trader, explaining that I was going to Algeria. Luckily, he knew about travel across the Sahara to North Africa. I soon found out there was a convoy truck scheduled to depart Gao for the city of Tamanrasset, in Algeria, in three days. This trip would be different because I would be sharing the ride not only with people, but also with livestock, goods and merchandise. The convoys that travel through the Sahara are not designed to transport human beings, but the drivers transport people in order to make extra money.

At this stage my resolve was tested. I was already apprehensive about my journey, and I had not factored in being a stowaway on a livestock convoy. As I stood on the sandy landscape of Gao with the desert wind blowing on my face, I noticed a group of women speaking to a trader on the side of the road in their local dialect. After they'd gone he said, "You see my friend? Many people want to ride this truck. It is safe for them. It is safe for you." To my surprise and astonishment, he spoke to me in broken but understandable English. How did he know I spoke English, and how did he know I was only passing through going to North Africa? He was truly my guardian angel watching and guiding over me. He pointed to an old man with white long white beard standing just a few feet away, saying that he would be the driver of the convoy. The old man explained he needed one more passenger in order to depart. I gathered with the other passengers in a mud brick house and waited for the old man to meet his passenger quota.

I had no idea how to physically prepare for the inhospitable desert environment. I finally began to understand the dangerousness of it when I watched the other passengers preparing for the trek. I soon realized that I needed quite a different kind of clothing than I'd worn in tropical West Africa. I was told I'd need a long cotton gown, from my shoulders to my feet, to withstand and endure the strong, dry wind with sand that is constantly blowing. I would also need a long, thick cotton head scarf. The scarf would be used to cover my head, ears and nose, protecting me from the cold, dry wind, leaving only my eyes exposed.

I stashed the traveler checks and my money in my waistband for safe-keeping, and purchased two fresh baked, long loaves of bread and canned sardines and jam. I wrapped the bread in plastic and placed all of the food inside my bag.

We were being transported in a huge, open air truck. Inside, a piece of metal divided the space into a compartment that separated the people from the livestock. There was also a big drum holding drinking water.

From Gao, the terrain becomes a no man's land, precisely as Tom had described it to me. As we drove further north towards the middle of the Sahara, I was shocked and amazed by the extreme vastness of the open space that extended far beyond the horizon, and by the fantastic features of the sand dunes. It took me some time to appreciate the beauty of the Sahara. Though inhospitable, the desert was a picturesque landscape, with beautiful browns, grays and rose tints woven into the sand. There was virtually no significant vegetation, only very few and scattered tundra trees that were extremely short in height and with virtually no leaves on them. The only significant and visible natural features were sand, dunes, and wind, and very high in the sky you could see the sun penetrating straight down. The dry wind blew constantly. The temperatures dropped below zero at night, and during the daytime, it was 120 or more. I quickly understood the necessity of the long gown and having my entire face wrapped as the sand blew through the open air truck.

The drive across the Sahara was long, arduous, and risky, undertaken only by experienced drivers. I distracted myself during the drive by thinking about how my life was now intersecting with the histories of captured Africans who were sold into slavery. I could not imagine how anyone could commit something as hostile as slave trading in a place like the Sahara, and further I couldn't imagine making the trip on foot. It would be certain death.

In the evenings we slept in the sand around the truck. When I looked up at night, the black skies were filled with fiery, twinkling stars—hundreds and perhaps thousands of brightly shining stars. They reminded me of the sparkling diamonds littering the ground that my people once thought were stars fallen from the sky. All I had to keep me warm in the freezing cold was the blanket I'd brought from Tom's house in Tamale. Sleeping on the sand was much like sleeping on the mat at Alfred's house; the cold sand was as unforgiving as concrete. I drew my knees into my chest and pulled my blanket all the way over my head, trying to escape the cold. My teeth would chatter as I drifted off into a fitful sleep. One night I dreamed I was being chased by a Bengal tiger. In the dream the tiger wanted my pocketbook. I ran through the desert winds trying to escape and then an orange tree appeared. I quickly climbed the branches to the top where I waited for the tiger to go away. I woke up with my heart racing. It was difficult to fall asleep each night.

Somewhere in the middle of the Sahara, I developed a debilitating high fever that made me very weak. I began to vomit inside the truck. My condition created quite a concern among my fellow passengers and the driver. Someone said that we were about three hours away from the town of Tessalit. I believe I fell ill due to the fluctuating temperatures and from drinking the water in the drum that was placed next to the livestock. I continued to vomit as the truck pierced through the thick Sahara sand and the gusting winds. The air felt freezing to me, even when the scorching sun was on high. I pulled my robe tight around my body. By the time the convoy arrived in Tessalit I was so weak that my fellow passengers had to lift me down from the truck. They laid me on the ground just outside the marketplace. As I lay sick in the sand in the middle of the Sahara, the convoy continued trekking through on to Tamanrasset without me.

As I lay in the sand, an old man with a long white beard dressed in a long robe suddenly appeared and stood over me. I heard him speaking to me in French. I sensed he knew I was helpless and terribly ill. I was so weak from fever that I was unable to respond. He continued to stand over me and extended his hands to me, grabbing both of my hands and pulling me to my feet. He asked me to come with him to his house, which was across from the transport depot.

When we entered the small house, I met his wife, who was also quite old. Two young men sat inside the two small bedrooms. After a while the woman brought me a hot meal. I still recall the fresh baked bread that came with her food. When I finished eating, she gave me some herbal liquid, which I drank without protest. The old man showed me to my sleeping area, and soon after I plunged into the deepest sleep I'd had since I left the house in Tamale.

The loudspeaker from the mosque awakened me with a start very early the next morning. Even though I was sick and weakened and felt on the brink of death, I still made sure my money was concealed in my pocket and in the waistband of my trousers with my belt over it. The dream about the Bengal tiger was reoccurring. I was definitely concerned about my health, but I also couldn't help feeling like losing all my money while attempting to cross the Sahara would be a type of death.

From the first night I spent with the family in Tessalit I began to feel better. My fever reduced, and I felt my strength returning. I could not explain why the old man had come to my aid and saved me. God's presence was almost tangible to me during this experience. I have a firm belief that God performs his marvelous tasks through people, and this family was being used to save my life. I felt the hand of God in my life, and I knew He would be with me as I proceeded through the desert, heading to unpredictable destinations along a treacherous path.

After two days with the old man and his family, my energy level was up, and I wanted to continue my journey. I had to wait three days for the next convoy to Tamanrasset. My biggest fear—because I did not have the visa to enter Algeria—was being sent back to West Africa through the desert. On the morning of the third day, the convoy arrived in Tessalit. The old man went with me to the departure point and asked the driver about the cost of the fare to Tamanrasset. Before I boarded the convoy, I went to the latrine behind the old man's mud-brick house to ease myself. In privacy, I took out money to give the old man and his wife for their generosity and care. I walked over to the veranda where the old man was waiting for me. I looked straight at him and handed him 2000 French francs. As the old man repeatedly thanked me, tears filled my eyes as I knew I would never see this family again.

The wife stood back but seemed to be attentively watching and listening. As I grabbed my bag about to walk towards the convoy, I sensed her approaching. I turned and reached out and grabbed both her hands. I bowed and thanked her. She embraced me while tears ran down my cheeks. I was a complete stranger, but they showed me love and kindness and saved my life. Unfortunately the old woman did not speak French so I was never able to speak to her, but she communicated with me with her care and generosity, love, kindness and compassion. It was truly an emotional parting.

The driver of the convoy was waving to me to come and board. I kept waving goodbye to the old man and his wife as they stood by and watched the convoy leave Tessalit for Tamanrasset.

My 3,000-mile perilous trek, which began some 35 years ago in Tamale, Ghana, and led me through the Sahara Desert to Tunis, is an adventure I still remember so clearly. I easily remember the towns of Segou, Mopti, Gao, Tessalit and Tamanrasset, so when the notorious terrorist group Al-Qaeda invaded and took over the city of Timbuktu and established a stronghold in the towns of Kindal and Tessalit, it hit home for me. When I saw on CNN that the towns of Timbuktu, Gao and Tessalit were under siege by terrorist groups linked to Al-Qaeda, and that the French military were engaging in bombing raids around Tessalit, I became quite emotional. It was as if I were back in Tessalit again after all these years. The attacks brought back 34 years of memories and it was, in my mind at least, as if no time had passed at all. I wondered if the old man and his wife were still living. If their sons had been caught in the conflict. Though I knew when I was leaving that I would probably never return, I still imagined that places like the village with mud brick houses with a veranda would always be in Tessalit.

During my time in the Sahara, thoughts about the ephemeral nature of villages, houses, and political structures were far from my mind. I knew leaving Tessalit that hurdles lay before me. I still remember thinking as I sat in the convoy headed for Tamanrasset how grateful I was that God had saved my life again. I placed the major obstacle that lay immediately ahead of me in God's hands. My faith was strong, but doubt is a pervasive thing. I wondered if God would again come to my rescue.

Chapter 7

IT TOOK ME another day and a half to reach the border of Algeria. The wind picked up, strong and dry. As we moved north I began to see vegetation again, a sign that the desert was perhaps not quite as severe in this region. The problem was that I did not have a visa to enter Algeria, which shares a border with Mali. Even though Algeria is in Africa, the people there consider themselves more Arab than Africans. In the southern part of the country they are light-skinned, and the further north you go towards the Mediterranean they more they look like European whites.

The driver of my truck had to smuggle me into Algeria. About a mile before the border checkpoint the driver told me and a few others with the same problem what to do. We were met by a tall Taureg man in a headdress with a walking stick. He led us into a small village where we stayed in a house for two days. We gave him some money, and on the second morning he took us a mile or so to a new truck which was waiting for us. I entered Tamanrasset, a big town in southern Algeria, at night. The people there spoke Arabic and French and I was able to communicate in the little French I knew. There were markets and bazaars and much to see, but I had to find my way to Algiers, the nation's capital on the Mediterranean in the north. I asked and learned about the bus to Algiers.

On the way we stopped in the towns of In-Salah, El-Golea and Ghardaia, and then I continued by bus to Algiers, arriving at night. I felt lost and lonely, but I was determined. In Algiers I wanted to convince myself that the hardest part of my travel was over because I had crossed the deadly Sahara Desert and only Tunisia lay between me and my final destination, Gioia Tauro in Italy. In spite of my temporary relief, I remained quite cognizant of my immediate fears and potential obstacles. What if an Algerian police officer stopped me and asked for my travel documents, and what if I were not allowed to enter Tunisia because I did not have a visa? As I worried about these issues, I reached out to check on the traveler's checks I had concealed in my waist band and I realized that they had been ruined by my excessive sweat in the desert. Everything inscribed on the checks was blurred and virtually unreadable, which made me panic. Luckily, and having heeded Tom's advice, I had kept the receipts for the traveler's checks inside the pages of my passport separately from the checks, concealed in a plastic purse with strings attached and tied to my neck. The receipts were not ruined, fortunately. Still, I worried about going into the bank to report my traveler's checks had been ruined and request another batch of checks because I did not have a visa to be in Algeria. What if the bank officials became suspicious of my claim and called the police? By that time I had spent all the cash I had.

It was now afternoon in Algiers. I stood underneath a tree next to a bus stop with my bag firmly in my hand and nowhere to go. For the first time since I'd left my friends and family, I truly felt cold and lonely in a city. As I watched people and traffic, I managed to say the Lord's Prayer and prayed God would keep me from being caught by Algerian police and sent back through the Sahara. I hesitantly walked into a bank and handed the bank official both my ruined checks and my receipt for the checks. The official took my ruined checks and the receipt and walked away, leaving me waiting at the counter. When she returned she asked for my passport and went into one of the offices.

As I waited for her return I continued to pray for God not to allow me to be caught in the country without a visa. I had devised a plan in my mind should I be questioned by police for not having a visa: I would say that I was only going through the country, and that I had a visa for Italy, my final destination. I hoped that explanation would be persuasive enough. While these other thoughts were racing in my head, the official returned with a smile on her face and handed me my passport and the receipts. She explained that the bank would have to wait for authorization from the

American Express Company in New York to issue me new checks in three days.

Tired and dirty, I walked out of the bank with my bag in my arms and by chance I met a French speaking Algerian youth. He was a student at the university and we got along well. He took me to the university dorm where I took a shower, got cleaned up, and very gratefully ate some free food. He gave me his address, as he wanted to keep in contact with me.

With my new checks in hand three days later, I obtained Algerian currency and purchased a train ticket for Tunis, from where I would take a boat to my final destination. I knew the obstacles ahead of me: first I had to go through Algerian customs, who would be bound to ask me why was I in their country without a visa, and then I would need to contend with the Tunisian customs who might not allow me to enter their country because I didn't have a visa. As these thoughts raged in my mind, I blamed myself for not using Tom's influence back in West Africa to help me obtain transit visas for Algeria and Tunisia. The train came to a stop at the Algerian border town of Souk-Aharas, but no custom guards came on board and after a while it continued towards the Tunisian border. Although Algeria and Tunisia were both African countries, they were indifferent to the fellow Africans south of the Sahara.

Upon entering Tunisia, the train stopped and the border guards came onboard checking travel documents. A female Tunisian border officer took my passport and continued checking passports. She came back and took me off the train into the office where I was detained for several hours because I did not have a visa to enter the country, even though I did have a visa to enter Italy. I was worried that I would be turned away and not allowed to continue my journey to my destination. My entire trip would be ruined, after having come so far! I realized that dark skinned Africans were treated differently than Arabs here.

In response to their questions, I argued that I had a visa for Italy, which I showed them. They questioned me further, wanting to know why I was traveling through Tunis. Why not just fly to Italy? Of course, I couldn't tell them that it was a personal challenge I had undertaken, that I needed to prove things to my friend and benefactor. But I did make what I hoped was a compelling case to them. They had initially wanted me to turn back, but I was steadfast in insisting that I only wanted to briefly pass through their nation and not actually stay there. Eventually and reluctantly they let me through. In total, I had been detained about six hours, long enough to have missed the train.

I did, however, take the next available train and arrived in Tunis. Once in the capital, I was sitting in a nice spot figuring my next move when I met a European fellow who was also traveling. His name was Mark, and he was from Bristol, England and he was going home. I began talking to him and he showed me how to get to the shipping company so that I could buy my ticket. I spent two nights in a youth hostel in Tunis waiting for the cruise ship to depart to Trapani on the island of Sicily.

When I first saw the cruise ship my eyes popped. I had never seen such a magnificent sight in my whole life. The only water conveyances I had ever seen were canoes and small ferries. This ship looked bigger than a mountain. It had three decks with a bar and dining rooms. It carried vehicles in the hold and even had, of all things, a swimming pool. I remained amazed during the whole crossing, which took all night. In the morning we arrived in Trapani and were boarded by Italian customs officials.

As a 21-year-old African young man I was fascinated by my new surroundings. Here I was in Europe for the very first time. I started to see an entirely different culture, complete with exotic foods like lasagna, spaghetti and wonderful pastries. I was thrilled to be standing on European soil. Yet the newness was a little scary, even as it was exciting. Through all of this, of course, I knew I had friends like Tom to back me, for which I was quite grateful. Moreover, I had begun to learn how to trust. I was lonely, yet I went ahead with confidence. I found the train station and had to wait, but I had my first Italian meal, a huge portion of lasagna and fresh baked bread, still warm. The train stopped in a town called Cefalu and I got out and sat at the café to wait for two hours for another train for my final destination, Gioia Tauro.

Everything was so different, with many cars whizzing about. People were happy. Many sang aloud in the streets. Everyone was saying "Ciao, amico."

I arrived in Palermo and for the first time I heard the word Mafia, though at the time I had no idea what it meant. Palermo was a large, bustling city with cars and buses everywhere. Some cars were big, though not as big as American cars. I knew little of the Italian cars except for the Alfa Romeo. Here the train stopped for an hour and then continued to Messina, which was the next big town. I noticed the Strait of Messina between Sicily and mainland Italy. They loaded the train onto a boat to cross over to the mainland at Villa San Giovanni, a town in Reggio Calabria. I was surprised and shocked that they were able to cut the train in half and drive it onto a boat. I watched the entire procedure in awe, and it took about 1 hour to complete the whole process.

The train conductor said in Italian that my stop was the next town. The train stopped in Gioia Tauro and I was the only passenger who got off the train. I walked up the stairs to the main street and with my bag in hand; I entered a bakery and asked in English how to get to the Park Hotel. The lady behind the counter screamed, and within a minute a man came out from the bakery shop dressed in white and with flour all over his hands. I sensed none of the family spoke or understood English. However, when I mentioned Park Hotel, they all pointed in the same direction.

I finally arrived at the hotel, but of course I didn't know this family. I was certain, however, that Stefano had either written to them or called them about me. Here I was, finally in Europe and about to reside with a family whose ways of life and culture were different from mine. I wondered whether the family was going to accept me, how would they treat and relate to me. As it would turn out, the Stanganellis were loving and absorbed me into their family, treating me with respect and dignity.

When I entered the Park Hotel, I heard a loud man's scream in the dining room area. I wondered if I had done something wrong. There was nobody at the hotel's reception counter. A young girl no more than 14 years old quickly appeared from behind the office. I cleared my throat and introduced myself. "My name is Francis and I am from Africa."

The girl shouted out loud and suddenly a woman came out from the dining room and said, "Si si, oh Stefano! Va bene, in Ghana, come stai. Si. Vine quai."

At that point, their son Tony, with his girlfriend beside him, tore into the parking lot in a little Alfa Romeo sports car. As he entered the hotel he said, "You are Francis from Africa? You know Stefano in Africa? Oh! Welcome, meet my father, Peppino."

I nodded shyly.

Two chefs dressed in white appeared and joined in the welcomes. I learned that the Park Hotel had three floors, with fifty rooms. Tourists came from all over Europe. Tony went and got a dictionary. He spoke a little English so we managed to communicate, though with a little difficulty. I learned that the older son was in Messina studying medicine. The family took me upstairs to the second floor and showed me my room. It was wonderful. The sheets were so white. That was the beginning of my life with the Stanganelli family.

Chapter 8

FOR A NEWLY arrived African youth, this experience living and working with the Stanganellis was the gateway to a whole new world. At first, of course, I was scared and lonely, but I was eager to learn and make my way. Adding to my anxiety was that I did not speak Italian. The Stanganelli family was generous and kind to me, which helped a lot. I often compared Peppino to cousin Alfred—the two were different in every way. After all the maltreatment I endured, I was now being bathed in affection.

One day soon after my arrival, I noticed that several people wandered into the hotel and stood staring at me without saying a word. I later learned that they were extended family members of Peppino and his wife, Anna Maria. I could appreciate their fascination, for I felt the same way. Here I was among a different type of white people with a culture and lifestyle unlike mine. It was an adventure and life experience beyond my wildest imagination.

My room was spacious and sparkling clean. On my first day Anna Maria came by my room, smiling, calling out, "Bien ca, Francesco." She then said, "Mange, mange." *Eat* in Italian, I was to learn. I followed her into the wide kitchen area beyond the dining room. There was an area designated for the hotel workers to eat, and on the table were three plates. One was full of steaming long white worms and another filled with red sauce. There was a plate of what looked like fried chunks of bread and freshly baked bread. Anna Maria pointed to her mouth and again said, "Mange,

mange." The only European food I had been exposed to was when I lived with Tom and Shauana in Tamale, Ghana. I was used to chicken, fish, vegetables, rice and legumes, but I never had seen anything like what was in front of me.

I stood there stupefied. I did not know what the food was, and parts of it did not look appetizing. All I recognized was the bread. For a while I sat at the dining room table looking at the food in front of me. Anna Maria came back to check on me and saw that I had not touched the spaghetti but had instead eaten the fresh bread with the sweet butter. The truth was I didn't know how to eat the spaghetti. With her daughter Bernadette at her side, Anna Maria brought a plate of spaghetti for herself and sat down and began eating. I watched how she ate, twirling the limp noodles on her fork. I was embarrassed at first, but after that first taste I became hooked on spaghetti for life.

I was introduced to the other employees. There were two chefs, one old female maid and one male waiter. My initial job description was quite vague. I was expected to be available to assist the cooks, particularly when there were wedding celebrations at the hotel. I would work in the kitchen washing the huge pots and performing other tasks. I also worked downstairs in the pastry shop where the pasta was made fresh, and I unloaded the daily truck deliveries and stocked the bar.

The family paid me a small stipend plus my room and board, including all the delectable Italian pasta dishes I could eat. There were also other perks. On days when I did not feel like doing anything it was perfectly fine with the family. As time went on, Peppino became fond of me and asked me to accompany him on errands to nearby towns and villages. His driver, Savalio, drove his brand new Alpha Romeo, and we would head out to the open road.

Initially, whenever I caught one of the family members staring at me it made me somewhat uncomfortable. But soon I understood that they were just curious since they had never dealt closely with a black person before. It was a learning situation for both of us, and I was so grateful to be there. After all, this family did not know me, and they were nevertheless taking the risk of absorbing a stranger, a young black man from Africa, into the midst of their closely knit family.

I learned a lot about them. Peppino, who was at that time in his early sixties, was a retired professional Italian soccer player and had amassed his wealth from that career. He owned a restaurant in Venice and an ice cream factory in Messina. His wife Anna Maria was a preschool teacher at a Catholic school in Gioia Tauro and was very religious. I saw her go to church carrying a fresh bouquet of flowers three times in a single week. The family had three children: Peppe, the eldest who was studying to become a doctor in nearby Messina; Tony, the younger brother who had dropped out of high school to assist his parents; and Bernadette, who was about fourteen.

The whole family lived in the hotel but they also had a villa in town that they frequently retreated to, particularly when Peppino and Anna Maria were arguing. It was a kind of escape valve, I guess. Their behavior often astounded me. During a peaceful gathering, the family would erupt into a heated argument with everybody shouting at one another and gesturing wildly with their hands. I wondered how such a loving family could engage in such loud arguments one minute and in the next display a truly genuine affection for each other. At times I felt a part of the family, but it took me a while to understand their ways. I came to understand that this type of communication was part of their culture, as Italians get quite passionate about many things, even though it's not always very pleasant to witness. What I liked most about them was that, much like in my culture, they valued family above all else.

Tony Stanganelli had dropped out of high school not only because he wasn't interested in it, but also because he wanted to become a soccer player like his father. Unfortunately, despite his passion for the sport he was not good enough. He had been relegated to substitute on his local town team. I frequently went with him to his games in and around town. Each week Tony would dress for the games, but he rarely played.

Eventually I came to know other Italians outside of the Stanganelli family. Mr. Quidor, a short man with dark hair, lived across the street from the hotel. He owned a two-story building where he made his home upstairs and operated a shoe store below. He had a connection with the shoe factory and exclusively sold men's leather shoes. I began going with him on

Sundays to sell shoes in a nearby town. The shoes were of high quality, and before long I found myself owning half a dozen pairs of fancy Italian shoes.

I remember thinking that my presence with Mr. Quidor at the various pizzerias in town provided a curiosity factor, which attracted people and helped sell shoes. Of course, I could have been wrong. I am certain that Mr. Quidor never intended to use me to sell shoes. The fact that our friendship led to increased sales was just a happy coincidence. I prefer to think that after travelling alone for some time, he needed a trusted associate, and on Sundays I was his man.

There was no denying, however, that I was the only black person in Gioia Tauro and a curiosity, if not a celebrity of sorts. Word had quickly spread in town about me working at the Park Hotel. At first when I walked downtown to the sandy beach people stared at me, and many shouted, "Ciao, ciao amico. Va bene." I heard this constantly from people on the street, and from those riding through town in their Alpha Romeos, Fiats, and on their Vespa mopeds. It made me uncomfortable to be so singularly noticed.

The longer I lived in Gioia Tauro the more I came to appreciate how they communicated. All the looks and greetings were meant as gestures of friendship. As I got to know several people around town I came to realize that this is how they broke the ice: eye contact, wide smiles, and friendly greetings. I still remember the first day I saw a white man in Sierra Leone. I was so curious, and I must have stared at him to no end. People in Africa reacted to Europeans in much the same way as these Europeans were reacting to me.

This dramatic enlightenment that I experienced in Gioia Tauro began to shape the way I felt about and viewed the world. I had already experienced so much and I had a burning desire to tell Tom that I had arrived at Gioia Tauro and was staying with the Stanganellis. I wanted to chat with him like we used to after school at the airport. I wanted to regale him with my stories so that he could share in my experiences, like we had done on so many occasions. So I sent Tom a telegram saying, "I have arrived safely in Italy and am living with the Stanganelli family in Gioia Tauro at the Park Hotel. Say thank you to Stefano." A few days later Tom replied, also via telegram, saying, "I am very proud of you. Be good. Be safe. Take care. Tom."

This telegram *thrilled* me and boosted my morale. Tom was proud of me? I hadn't been able to articulate what I wanted most out of our relationship, but when I read his words, "I am very proud of you," I knew that Tom's pride in me was exactly what I'd been hoping for. Tom's confidence in me told me that he could see the benefits of the money he'd paid for my education. I was worthy of the time, the attention, the investment. I was on top of the world.

I felt relieved and happy that I had reached my final destination after making such an arduous trek through the Sahara. I believed that I made it to my destination through the grace of God and through the moral support and inspiration and encouragement of friends like Tom and Stefano. While roaming the streets of Gioia Tauro, I would turn over my travel experiences in my mind. I wondered what would have happened if I had been caught being smuggled into Algeria? Or what if they had detained me a lot longer at the Tunis border? What if I had been sent back to West Africa through the Sahara Desert again? Would I have survived a second trip? Being sent back would have undermined all my ideas of a challenge, of the rite of passage I had built up in my mind and my heart. I would have rather died in the desert than to have been sent back.

Soon I wanted to explore the nearby areas in Sicily. I was particularly fond of the ship called the Strait of Messina. It reminded me of the cruise liner on which I sailed in from Tunis. The more I explored, the more I liked Sicily. Though I was alone, I felt quite content. I often took a train from Gioia Tauro to visit towns like Paterno, Catania, Taormina and Messina.

My ultimate goal was still to reach the United States. My general plan was to work with the Stanganelli family and wait for Tom to visit me in Italy. My life plan changed when I met a German woman, a tourist by the name of Gaby Klugg who had come to Italy on vacation and was staying at the Park Hotel. One day I was in the basement cleaning the pastry machine in preparation for the next wedding when a waitress came down and asked me to help a busload of tourists with their luggage. At that time I couldn't tell one European from another; Germans, Dutch, Danes and Swiss all looked alike to me. As Peppino and Bernadette checked each guest into the hotel, I ran the luggage upstairs. The guests all seemed very excited to be at the hotel. There were young and old tourists in the group and they were all very polite to me.

Later that same day I was standing behind the counter with Peppino when a short woman with dark shiny hair said hello to me in English. Her body language suggested that she wanted to converse with me. She told me she was German and asked me where in Africa I was from. She wanted to continue the conversation even as she waited to conduct business at the counter.

The conversation with this woman made me uncomfortable because it appeared that I may have been singled due to the color of my skin. Peppino threw me some kind of a glance, a smile, but I had no idea what it meant. I briefly relayed the high points of my story to her. When she left she said, "Bye, see you later." I hadn't gotten her name, but I found it on the tourist check-in card. Later I was working the bar with Tony when she came up, sat down and asked for a glass of water. She started yet another conversation with me. I was a bit timid and reluctant, and I don't think she realized I wasn't really interested. Not that she wasn't attractive; I just didn't want to jeopardize my position at the hotel and with the family in any way. I let her do most of the talking. She spoke mostly about her vacations and travels.

I was indeed conflicted. I longed for someone to talk to and here was this woman speaking to me at length in English, but I also cherished my connection to the hotel and couldn't risk unprofessionalism. All of this was further complicated by the fact that I was still an innocent and had no experience with women. I had noticed a young Italian girl about my age each time I walked through town or on my way to the beach. She was always alone on her red Vespa motorbike. Each time she saw me she gave a friendly wave and called, "Ciao, Francesco, ciao," and then she sped off. I thought and hoped she might like me. Before I met Gaby, pursuing a relationship with any woman was the furthest thing from my mind, though I must admit that I very much fancied this Italian girl. I wondered if she would ever date a black man. I doubted it, but I still hoped. How could I possibly converse with her? I still dreamed and fantasized about her.

Aside from these dalliances into fantasy, my main hope was to see Tom again. My longtime desire to go to America was as strong as ever, but

Gaby would make me an offer that would be difficult to turn down. Oftentimes when Gaby attempted to carry on a conversation with me we would be interrupted. On one occasion Tony made several attempts to interrupt our conversation, but she ignored him and finally got up and went to join her tour group for dinner. The next day Gaby asked me to take a walk into town with her for a coffee, followed by a walk on the beach. She phrased it in such a way that it was almost impossible to refuse. We visited a café and I had by now developed a liking for cappuccino. We attracted a lot of stares. People even honked their horns at us, which irritated her. She said those people were ignorant, crude and stupid. People still called out to me, "Ciao, ciao, Francesco." For the happy young Italians, my walking in town with a white woman was apparently a hot topic of curiosity.

As Gaby and I continued to get to know each other better, I learned of her love of travel, culture and anthropology. Moreover, she had a strong interest in me, my people, my village, our culture and Africa in general. She related that she once took a class on African dancing. Now that, to me, was odd. As we walked along the beach I learned of the Northern European love of the sun, something they don't see that much of, thus their yearly vacation migrations to the south. She called it "hunting" for the sun, and she said most northerners loved to lie in the sun all day.

By the time we got back to the hotel, just what I didn't want: word of our "romantic" excursion, had already happened. By now the whole family had begun to notice her interest in me and this made me very uncomfortable. That evening Peppino told me that he wanted me to work the front reception desk for the night just in case some clients came in late. I was relieved, because I expected him to be angry about my going out with Gaby. Gaby found me at the front desk and chatted me up, telling me that she was leaving in the morning, and she gave me her contact information. I thought to myself that this might be the last time I saw her. She said it was only goodbye for now.

About two weeks later I got a phone call from Gaby. I was in the kitchen with Chef Nino. Bernadette came into the kitchen area and picked up the phone and waved it in my direction saying, "Pronto, pronto." I had never received a phone call at the hotel before. I thought and hoped it was Tom, but I heard Gaby's voice saying, "Hello, Francis. How are you?" As we spoke all eyes were fixated on me. I was thinking that I might have to cut the conversation short, not only because other calls were coming in but also because I was embarrassed. I hoped that I didn't appear rude to her, but I was sure she thought so. Two days later I took a train to Messina to the Italian Government Phone Exchange where I could talk to her with privacy. I sensed that she was excited to hear from me. She had plenty of time to talk, but I had only paid for thirty minutes. She explained how to make a collect call and implored me to phone her collect the next week at the same time.

Oddly enough, on the train ride home, as I relaxed to the sound of the click-clacking wheels, my mind began to drift back to Punduru. I wondered how soon I would see my mother and family again. My mother was quite advanced in age, and I was worried about seeing her before she passed. These were some of the bittersweet thoughts that frequently came over me while I was in Italy.

The next time Gaby and I spoke, she began talking about travel in Europe and about how easy and cheap it was to travel on a Eurail pass and use youth hostels all over Europe. I told her my plan was to remain with the Stanganelli family until Tom came to help me get a visa for school in America. Gaby was single-minded in her conversation about travel. She came right out and said she wanted to see me again at the hotel. I'm not sure how mysterious the silence was, but all I could do was hold the phone for several seconds. I could sense her own hesitance. Finally she asked, "Are you still there, Francis?"

I blurted out, "I'm living with Peppino's family, and I don't want anything to jeopardize my relationship with them." At the same time I relayed to Gaby that I very much wanted to get to know her. And I went further, which was bold for me, hinting that I wondered how she felt about me. Gaby's answer was rather indirect; she went on about how beautiful and rich in history the towns and villages in Sicily were, and how much there was to do. I told her I, too, would love to see all these places.

I don't know if it was a spur of the moment decision, but Gaby informed me that she was coming to Sicily, but this time on her own. I sensed that she had been to Sicily many times before. We had a brief discussion about the Mafia, which she said had begun in Palermo before spreading around the world. Before the call ended I reminded her that she wasn't to call me at the hotel and that I would call her. She ended the conversation with a German farewell. "Auf Wiedersehen, meaning see you later." After that call I began to wonder if the Stanganelli family was involved in the Mafia, but I didn't dare ask Tony about it.

The next time Gaby and I spoke, she had just come in from work. She was a pharmacist and she was complaining about how much she disliked her job. She expressed a dream to be free and to travel and see remote places. Since time was limited I asked what her plan was, and she quickly related to me, "Francis, I am coming to Messina in three weeks, I want you to travel with me around Sicily."

There it was. I felt like I knew Gaby well enough, and I had feelings for her, yet I worried about my commitment to the Stanganelli family. I had grown very fond of Gaby, and she knew it. Still, I wondered why this white German woman who was about ten years or so older than me was so interested in me.

I was afraid of the family's reaction. I had seen how they dealt with conflict and I could not imagine myself yelling back at anyone in the family. I knew the relationship was not a secret. They'd gotten an inkling of the attraction between us months earlier. For some reason the subject of the Mafia again intruded on my mind, and before I got to the subject of Gaby and me I was determined to get an answer. I went up to Tony one day and bluntly mentioned the word. He looked at me and laughed as he raised his right thumb and made a sign along his right jaw as if his right thumb was a knife cutting his cheek. Tony did not speak English except a word here and there, so it was difficult to press him to explain. But I sensed Tony's meaning. His answer was something that I learned was quite common and cultural, and that was to deny the existence of such an organization of criminals. One time Anna Maria heard us discussing it. She approached us, raised her hand up under her chin and flicked her fingers saying, "No Mafia," and she quickly walked away into the kitchen.

My real problem, telling the family about travel with Gaby, ultimately overshadowed whether or not there really was a Mafia.

Chapter 9

I WAS IN the kitchen when Gaby arrived. Peppino was at the reception desk, but he didn't recognize her from her last visit. She asked for me, and Peppino yelled my name. When I got there I saw her with a big smile on her face. Tony, Anna Maria, Bernadette, and some guests in the lobby were all staring at me. My emotions were churning. I was so excited to see her, but I was embarrassed that she'd come to the hotel. She assured me she was staying at the nearby Mediterranean Hotel.

When I finished working for the day, I met up with Gaby and we took a walk to the beach. It was late afternoon. By now the townspeople knew me very well, so they no longer honked their horns as we walked along. I waved at the young Italian girl when she drove by, but she did not wave to me. I was beginning to have feelings for Gaby, but I was still rather reserved. I restated my feelings about the Stanganellis and about getting with Tom in order to go to America. These talks helped us grow closer as friends. I opened up to her about my cruel cousin Alfred. She was the first person I ever shared the details of the abuse I'd endured with. Although I wanted to be with her, I was still hesitant.

As we approached the beach Gaby wrapped her arms around my neck and said, "Travel with me, Francis. We'll hop around Sicily. We could have such big fun." My heart started to pound. I don't know how long I was frozen in silence. I just kept walking. As we approached the sand she said, "Take your shoes off," and slipped her shoes off. Walking along the shoreline, she kept dipping her feet into the water.

I told her, "Gaby I appreciate the telephone calls. The collect calls and all." It's all I could come up with. The tension in my stomach melted away when Gaby grabbed my hand. We walked along hand in hand, watching the sunset along with tourists who were still lingering on the beach.

"I've told my mother about you. I even told her about how I want to see Sicily with you." I became acutely aware of our differences in that moment. I studied her white hand in mine and started thinking about her proposition. I understood why Tom took an interest in me; he wanted to help a poor African boy. I was also lucky in getting the position with the Stanganellis. They had welcomed me into their family. But now with Gaby I wondered. What was her interest in me? I struggled to understand what she expected from me.

Nevertheless, I counted meeting Gaby as more good luck. I did not want to miss the opportunity to see more of the world, especially while spending time with Gaby. I blurted out, "Gaby, how do I explain this to Peppino, us and my leaving with you? What if Tom showed up and I was nowhere to be found? I would miss an opportunity to go to the United States." Gaby rolled her eyes. In retrospect she may have been a little impatient with my naiveté. To my view at the time she was asking to do something that might derail my life plan, ruin my life.

She said, "Tell them 'I met a friend, and I want to travel with her. I'll stay in touch and let everyone know where I am.'"

I played a scene of the conversation with Peppino in my mind. I imagined him giving me his blessing. I immediately started preparing a mental list of things to do in preparation for departure, and my daydream came to a screeching halt when I got to finances. I asked, "How am I going to travel with no money?"

She giggled and said, "Not to worry, my friend. I want to travel in Sicily and spend time with you. The money will come when we need it." She released my hand and went to the edge of the water and made a dance of splashing her feet in the water of the Tyrrhenian Sea. So there it was: all she expected was the chance to get to know me better. My hesitation was diminishing. I asked myself, *Should I go with this woman to Sicily?* As I watched her dance at the shoreline a thought came from way in the back of my mind: What if we run into the Mafia? Sicily is a large place, and will likely be home to the Mafia. What if someone tries to rob Gaby and me of our money? I did not want to be stranded in Sicily with no money. That was not a conversation I wanted to have with Tom.

I told myself that I had to take the risk if I wanted to go on this adventure. By then I had learned that taking adventures to unknown places always comes with risks. I decided to do it, although I didn't like the idea of giving up my clean room and three great meals per day, and my relationship with the family and my friends in town. I would be trading all this just to go with Gaby, who I really didn't know too well. I played out a scenario in my mind, one where we break up in the hills of Italy and I'm left having to make yet another journey to Gioia Tauro. Would the Stanganellis take me back? I told the Stanganellis about my plans and that I wanted to keep in touch. When I mentioned the idea of one day returning to the Park Hotel, Peppino simply said, "Anytime, Francesco." I told the family everything about Gaby and they all wished me well.

When I broke the good news to Gaby she was so excited that she went out and bought me a backpack for my shoes and clothes, saying, "We could leave right now. Oh, Francis. What big fun we are going to have together." I couldn't think of any reason not to start our journey right away, so I said yes to her, and goodbye to the family. The day I left I saw a strange look on Anna Maria's face, almost like she was saying *don't go*. I fought the tears that welled up in my eyes. This was the second time in my life that I was saying goodbye to my family. I truly felt like a son, brother, cousin and friend among the Stanganellis, just like I was son, brother, uncle, cousin and friend in my family and among my village community. Looking into Anna Maria's eyes deflated my heart for a moment as the reality of leaving 'home' yet again came crashing down on me. It was difficult to break Anna Maria's stare, but Peppino's booming voice did the work for me. He patted me on the back and said, "Go, go."

Gaby and I hopped a train the next morning for Messina. I had traveled to Messina with Peppino on multiple occasions, but Gaby promised to show me a side of the town that I never saw with Peppino. After that, the next time we got off the train near Catania, Gaby said we were going to visit a town called Taormina. She said it had one of the most fantastic beaches on Sicily, a quiet place where we could have the beach to ourselves, unlike the overcrowded beaches in Gioia Tauro, where American tourists could be found year round.

To get down to the beach in Taormina we would have to take an electric cable car which ran on wires suspended in the air above ground. This was the first time I had ever seen anything like this. Gaby and I stood waiting among the European tourists who were also waiting to catch a ride down to the beach. The passengers emptied out of the car and the new set, including Gaby and I, loaded in. I sat next to Gaby as the car lifted from the ground towards the electric cables and began to move. I watched our descent from the top of a very steep mountain over a rugged terrain towards the beach far down below.

The communication between Gaby and me during the five minute ride down to the beach was nonverbal. As I frantically kept gazing outside through the glass windows, I turned with wide eyes and looked at Gaby. She responded by staring back at me, opening her eyes as wide as possible without blinking, and with a huge smile planted on her face. She sat there with the strange look on her face for several seconds. As we exited the car, Gaby immediately grabbed my hands and burst into silly laughter while shaking her head. We walked along the beaches of Taormina holding hands.

On our first night in Catania, Gaby and I had a lovely dinner of manicotti and fresh baked bread. We went over the details of our trip thus far and she listened as I marveled over the cable car. That night after dinner, Gaby and I went to bed early. Where I was still shy and timid, Gaby was bold, shrewd and aggressive.

The next day Gaby announced that there was a volcano on the island of Sicily, at Mount Etna. She said she wanted to show me the hotel in Etna. Geography was one of my favorite subjects. My mind drifted back to my studies of rocks, ocean currents and volcanoes. I remembered all the details of volcanoes. How the earth cracks, causing hot molten lava up to the surface. I was sold on the chance to see and experience a volcano with my own eyes. The experience of Mount Etna far surpassed reading about volcanoes. Mt. Etna was huge. I saw hot vapor venting from the very top of the rocky peak. I watched several European tourists wield long lens cameras as they captured photos of the eruptions. It was amazing. Here I was at the foot of Mt. Etna watching one of the most amazing events on earth. The mountain erupted with bright red lava covered in ash. The tide of rocky-red lava flowed down the mountain's side and cooled in lava fields. Amazing.

Gaby said that our next stop would be Greece, a country that I knew very little about. I knew some ancient history, but that was all. I knew more about the French, American, and Russian revolutions and European history. I wondered about Greece. What was there for us to see? Wouldn't I need a visa? But I was enjoying getting to know Gaby, and I was growing fonder of her, her warmth, her charm, her friendship. She was the type of woman I came to know as a no-nonsense German. She was blunt and bold, yet shrewd and very nice. She had no patience for stupidity. She told me that of all the people she had come in contact with from nations around the world, Americans were by far the most materialistic and wasteful. I did not understand what she meant by materialistic. I reminded her of my friend and benefactor who was American. I pointed to his generosity and how he had earned my respect. She told me that she came to know Americans from the military in Germany and was not too fond of them. But nothing could convince me to agree with her on the topic of Americans' character. Back in Africa we liked Americans. Who we didn't like too well were the British. I'm sure she understood my position as a poor African who got lucky.

I enjoyed talking to Gaby about everything from history to culture to nature. I was confused, however, about our travel arrangements. My visa to Italy had expired, and I wondered how I would get into Greece on an expired visa. I shared these concerns with Gaby. Inasmuch as I wanted to be with her and travel, I was not interested in another crisis at the border. Gaby told me not to worry, she was confident I would get a visa. We set out by train, headed straight for Rome. The train ride took at least eight hours. When we arrived in Rome we immediately headed to the Greek consulate. Gaby convinced the official that she had adequate funds and that I was traveling with her. I think the reason the consulate was so accommodating was that Greece had just joined the EU, of which Germany was an important part; Gaby was German, and they gave me a three-month visa. To celebrate we visited the Vatican in Rome, which was indeed a spectacular sight to behold.

There were lots of Americans in Rome. I recognized their American English from listening to Tom talk. All of the Americans looked well dressed and wealthy. I spoke to one American in a café. I was eager to know where he was from. I told him I was preparing to go to America. He told me he was from Boston and that he was traveling on the Interrail pass. He described the pass as a cheap tourist's ticket to travel throughout Europe. And any places the Interrail pass could not get him, hitchhiking could. I balked at the notion. Where I am from, you do not get in a car with strangers. He assured me that in Europe hitchhiking was safe, respectable and, of course, free. After talking with the young American I decided to join Gaby and the college kids and hitchhike around Europe ... but not before exploring Rome more.

Rome was fascinating. I saw it as ancient Rome come to life in the modern world. Gaby and I walked into St Peter's Square, where I gazed in awe at the array of fantastic statues. I was amazed by the Swiss Guards in their colorful medieval uniforms. I saw members of the Pope's personal army and his body guards. I was disappointed that we did not have time to visit the Sistine Chapel, but we were in a hurry to get on to Brindizi to start our Greek adventure. Gaby convinced me we could find work in Greece while we explored and saw the sites. We took the train to the outskirts of Rome, and we were going to hitchhike to Brindizi on the east coast of the Adriatic Sea. I still didn't really understand hitchhiking. Initially, when she told me what hitchhiking was, I got mad and wanted to return to Gioia Tauro. How dare she expect me to sit by the road and beg for a ride? She reminded me that hitchhiking provided the perfect means to achieve our travel goals, and a way to experience the people and the countryside.

Gaby bought some fresh bread, salami and cheese. We had bottled water, and between rides we sat down to eat. Eventually I caught on to the rhythm of hitchhiking. Gaby preferred it while she stood at the edge of the road with her arm and thumb outstretched. I would watch her, squinting in the sun and think, *sure hitchhiking is good enough for the American tourist, so it's good enough for me.*

The first time we were out trying to catch a ride, a car with a man and a woman stopped. When Gaby signaled me to come along, the driver pulled off. Luckily another car stopped, and they were friendly. The driver helped us put our luggage in the back. He spoke a little bit of English and asked, "Americans? Military?"

Gaby said, "No, I'm German."

I said, "I am from Africa."

The man said, "Oh." Then there was a long silence. I sensed that if we weren't already underway, he probably would not have given us a ride. We hitched from town to town, and we even got rides on trucks. Once when I was mistaken for an American by an Italian truck driver, Gaby lost her patience, answering for me saying, "No, he is from Africa."

It was a long, arduous trip. Hitchhiking is by no means glamorous. Though it may be respectable in that part of the world, it could never be my first choice for travel. Along the road I learned that I am more flexible than I thought. I interacted with total strangers and began to feel at home while on vacation. The huge amount of fun I was having, combined with my growing affection for Gaby, competed with my anxiety over the possibility of missing the opportunity to meet up with Tom in Italy. Oftentimes riding in the cars I would imagine that the driver was taking me to Tom. I pictured a tearful goodbye with Gaby, and boarding an airplane headed for America.

Chapter 10

OUR LAST RIDE took us all the way to the port of Brindizi, where we were going to catch a cruise ship to cross the Adriatic Sea to Greece. I was ambivalent again, wondering if I had made a mistake. I missed my nice room and the three terrific meals a day at the Park Hotel. I was also fearful for my personal safety. I think Gaby knew I was worried. After all, I was going to a country I did not know much about, and it had all happened rather unexpectedly. We had become intimate, but still I worried about my future, regardless of the excitement of the new passion.

The idea of standing by the road waiting for a ride continued to make me uncomfortable. I was so against it that at times I threatened to return back to Gioia Tauro. I often wondered if she knew I was just bluffing. I still wanted to be with her. Every day I was learning new things about Gaby. I had, for example, noticed that wherever we traveled she liked to pay special attention to the aesthetics, the beauty of the land, the people, and the wildlife. It didn't make much sense to me, but I was a newcomer to Europe. I felt lucky to be with her, despite my worries.

Gaby also liked to distinguish the different songs of the birds. She was always exclaiming, "Look. Look. Listen. Listen to the sounds of the birds." This caused me to flash back to my early days in my village when I used to drive birds away from the rice fields. I could not fathom the significance of her love of birds singing. It seemed strange and weird to me at that time.

I gave her an ultimatum. I told her, "I will not hitchhike in Greece. If that's your plan, then I'm going back." She assured me we would not hitchhike in Greece.

I found myself on a cruise ship again, at least as large as the last. This brought me back to my other crossings, the River Niger in West Africa, the Mediterranean Sea from Tunis, the Straits of Messina in Italy, and now the Adriatic Sea. I was eager to write to Tom to tell him all that I was doing. I was worried that he might conclude I no longer needed him because I had a girlfriend and had left the Stanganellis.

Gaby and I departed Italy in the evening and arrived in Patras, Greece the next morning. There were lots of youths with backpacks on the ship, European kids who were happy and friendly. There were a number of hippies among them, and I heard American English. There were sleeping berths below, but Gaby and I slept on deck. By now I had my own sleeping bag.

During the trip I wrote Tom a letter. I also wanted to send a telegram to tell him I was not in Italy, as I suspected that by now Stefano knew I had left the Stanganellis. My biggest dream, which I would not allow to pass me by, was to go to America. I was getting close enough to Gaby that I knew it would be difficult to leave her when the time came. As for her, in retrospect I have come to realize that she was emotionally strong and understood how to handle the sadness of parting.

Gaby had been to Greece before and fell in love with the people and the history. Everything was quite strange for me and I did not speak Greek. I noticed that the Greeks looked much like the Italians. There weren't, however, as many fancy cars racing down the streets of Greece as there were in Italy. I sent the telegram to Tom describing my situation and mentioning that I had written him a letter to explain everything.

Then Gaby and I went to the local bank to exchange our German marks into the Greek currency, the drachma at the time. As we talked, I continued learning more about her; she once told me she wanted to visit Africa and go on a safari because she loved the animals in the jungle. I must admit I thought that was strange, and I wondered about her. All I knew from my life in Africa was that animals were dangerous.

We took a bus to the ancient and legendary town of Olympia. I'd learned that the Greeks started the original Olympic Games, originating in the very place we were standing. I gazed in awe at the Temple of Hera, from where the Olympic flame is lit and taken all over the world during the Olympic Games. Here I was, standing at the birthplace of ancient history. I felt an odd oneness with the place as I walked around examining the centuries-old site. I could see all the antiquities that I had studied right before my own eyes. What remained, of course, were only rubble and boulders, and I wondered why so many tourists were taking pictures of stones and rubble. I was usually the only black person at these sites, though it really didn't make me uncomfortable. By this time, after living with Tom in the upper class neighborhood and the Stanganellis in a tourist location, I had grown accustomed to being the only black person. I met so many nice people and formed so many genuine friendships that the differences in skin color faded to the background of my thoughts.

We stopped in Athens to stand at the site of the Acropolis, the center of civilization, where democracy was born. We went through the city of Corinth and I gazed at the canal that separates Greece into two sections. I wondered if this waterway's history was as long and rich as the history of the River Niger. Gaby and I often talked about history and culture as we walked around in Athens. At times it was like having a personal tour guide. We sat holding hands at the Syntagma Square overlooking the Greek parliament and watched the parade and changing of the Royal Greek Guards.

I had my first Greek meal in a tavern—souvlaki, which is meat roasted over a fire, as well as a Greek salad with lots of feta cheese, olives and fresh tomatoes. There was lots of tobacco smoke inside the tavern. Greek men were drinking Turkish coffee and playing cards and dominoes. There were a few Europeans sitting outside. The whole thing looked like a scene from a travel guide. While the food was delicious, the experience paled in comparison to my introduction to Italian food. I much preferred the pasta dishes with rich cheeses and tomatoes stewed, roasted, or sun dried. I tasted the best honey that I have ever eaten in my life while visiting Greece.

On the train to Argos, we met lots of friendly European backpackers, Germans, French, British and others. Gaby told me there was work to be found on the Greek farms picking oranges, olives and apricots in the area surrounding the town of Nafplio. Since Greece had just joined the European Economic Community (EEC), the Greek market was now opened up to the rest of Europe. The demand for Greek produce was so great that there was now a huge demand for labor on the farms. We ran into several European migrant workers who had the same idea. The migrant workers weren't, however, migrant workers in the traditional sense of the term. They were mostly young travel enthusiasts who were venturing out into the world. They were college kids, or recently graduated, who were traveling for fun and saw Greece as a perfect holiday destination to enjoy the sunny climate and cheap wine.

I came to know an American youth named Matthew. He spoke Greek very well, as he was studying in Athens. Since Matthew was American, I told him of my plans of going to America to further my education. In response, he wrote to his father who later sent me an application for admission to Springfield Community College, in Springfield, Massachusetts. Once again it seemed that a new opportunity might be knocking at my door.

Chapter 11

GABY AND I settled in Assini, a village near Nafplio. The closest nearby city was Argos, which is featured in legendary Greek mythology. All the northern Europeans who arrived by car drove through Assini on their way to Tolon. The village of Tolon is a beautiful coastal beach town popular with tourists, with camping sites and hotels and restaurants. Tolon and Argos could not be more different. One is devoted to farming and the other to fun. I stayed away from Tolon during the tourist season.

I got to know a lot of the farmers in Assini as well as a very big landowner named Yorogos Christopolos-Vangelis. I soon developed a reputation as one of the hardest workers in the area. I could withstand the hot sun better than the Europeans. I was quick and efficient loading fruit racks unto trucks, and I climbed the olive trees faster, too. At this time Greek agriculture was booming, so there were always empty trucks waiting to be loaded with oranges and other produce for transport to the Northern European markets.

When one work season ended another began. After the orange picking season ended, then came the demand for olives. Before I knew it months had passed, and Gaby and I were still together and still in Greece. We picked olives together, which is much harder than picking oranges. Southern Greek olive trees are usually high, which requires the use of ladders and spreading nets underneath the trees. You have to climb the tree and comb the olives off the branches. The Greek farmers came to know me as a skillful tree climber. I would climb the olive trees to the very top and make sure all the olives were picked. After my childhood climbing orange and kola trees, I climbed with such natural dexterity that it amazed the farmers. This earned me many accolades among the farmers of Assini and even beyond.

Grape picking is even harder than olive picking. The vineyard trees are thick and the task requires that you bow them down. I worked in a few vineyards where I was able to pick the grapes standing straight up, but this was not the norm. When those seasons were over, the planting of young orange trees was next. This is a time-sensitive task; the young seedling trees have to be planted before the rain starts to fall. Farmers usually want to plant their new trees quickly and then begin the task of irrigating the newly planted trees. I dug hundreds of holes in contoured strips of hard, rocky soil. This job was quite laborious, and I found that most of my European friends did not have the stamina for performing arduous labor under the hot Mediterranean sun.

If I wasn't picking oranges, grapes, or olives, or digging holes for orange trees, then I was cutting grass in the orange fields. The tools used were similar to those I had used for many years in Punduru, back in Sierra Leone, and I found adapting my skills to the Greek farm easy. I learned to use a sickle to cut grass so well that I came to be known for doing an excellent job, leaving farmers satisfied every time. The farmers called me George, a common male Greek name. I found this funny.

My reputation grew to the point that Greek farmers in Assini actively sought me out. I found myself negotiating for my wage for whatever tasks were to be done. They would call out to me, "Hey, George, I want you to plant my new orange trees." Always I'd respond, "How many?" An average job required digging approximately three hundred holes. I still recall one particular incident involving a farmer named Panayotis, who desperately needed 150 boxes of sweet mandarins picked immediately for his supplier. It was raining that day and Panayotis could not find anybody who was up to the challenge, so he sought me out. I told him how many drachmas I wanted to pick the 150 boxes. He paid me 3,000 drachmas, which was about two and one half times my usual daily pay of 1,200 drachmas.

To prepare for the job, after putting on my plastic boots I took two straight shots of fine Greek ouzo, and off I went to the rainy fields. Thank

God the trees were short enough that I did not have to climb them, and the mandarins were big enough that they quickly filled the individual plastic boxes. Within two hours I had picked a hundred boxes. I had developed a state of mind that allowed me to mentally block out the rain and the cold, and I was picking with all my heart and spirit.

Before another two hours were up, Panayotis came with the tractor. I had already exceeded 150 boxes. When he saw all the boxes filled to the brim, he said in awe, "Calos, calos … pedia … poly feresos," meaning, "Good, good boy. Thank you very much." Now I had the daunting task of taking all the boxes from the field and loading them onto his tractor, by myself. My adrenaline was already pumping, and I completed that task in approximately 30 minutes.

Aside from the picking and planting, there was also work with irrigation ditches in the orange fields. I'd either irrigate a new field or divert a trench to other fields. I traveled as far as Peloponnese, where irrigating orange fields was done almost all year round.

One only had to show up early in the morning at a café called Takis, where the Greek farmers came in the mornings on their tractors, pickups, and on donkeys, looking for laborers. The wage was negotiated on the spot, and the farmers fed the workers during the day. There was so much work you could work for the same family for weeks or months. I also came to know the migrant workers in Assini and they knew me as well. I became the go-to person when looking for work on a farm in Assini. I found that most of the workers came to have fun. I doubt that any of them saved any money. It was common to see the day's wages spent on alcohol and food, even though food and wine were cheap. I think I had a different attitude about my labor on the farm compared to the other migrant workers. I suspect for them their time in Greece was really about sun, surf and fun, while I envisioned saving as much as I could for the journey to America that I had prayed to God for. I had fun, too, but I could not see myself living hand to mouth again.

I knew every Greek family in Assini, and I had learned how to hold basic conversations in Greek. At first they were curious to see a black man in their midst. My landlord Yorogos told me they'd never before had a black man in their village. Yorogos let me stay in a little farmhouse on his orange farm, which became the center for the migrant workers. There were always people hanging around our farm house, and at one point Gaby said she didn't like it. She and I shared one room and the other bedroom was a community room. It was never quiet in the house; there was always a lot of drinking ouzo and Greek wine, and cooking using dried orange trees, which burned very slowly.

Even as I found myself standing in the midst of it, and being physically present and seeing Greek history, art, culture, mythology, etc. with my own eyes, I still didn't grasp the inherent significance of the ancient civilization that once stood where I was now living. It didn't really make any difference to me until years later when I came to the United States and took "History of Western Civilization" in college. Only then did I have a moment of clarity, and developed an appreciation for the tremendous opportunity I'd had to witness ancient history that had had such a profound impact on the modern world. I marveled at the fact that Turks used Greeks as slaves; when Greece broke from bondage, they in turn discriminated against women and slaves. Women and slaves were excluded from participating in civic and political affairs. Yet the democratic principles, ideas, concepts and practices that originated from Greece soon spread throughout the world, in spite of its cultural imperfections. I realized that no country is immune to the challenges and struggles that come with intermixing cultures.

I knew of the numerous Greek islands, but never had a desire to visit any of them. I was quite comfortable in the village of Assini where I was friends with virtually each and every family. I also came to know several Greek fishermen in Assini who owned taverns along the beaches and in nearby villages. Summer in Greece was a time of merriment, especially along the beaches of Tolon and Drepanon. The restaurateurs fried freshly caught fish and calamari and prepared Greek salads with lots of fresh cucumbers, tomatoes, olives, and feta cheese to accompany any order. The variety of Greek wines, along with the healthy dishes, added to my summer merriment.

Although hundreds of tourists came from Germany, France, Sweden, England, Denmark and Switzerland to lie on the beaches, I could never understand why anyone would take pleasure in sun bathing. There were other lures to the beach. I was introduced to snorkeling in the aqua blue waters of the Mediterranean, and it became my favorite pastime. Whenever I wasn't working I was always at the beach snorkeling. I stayed in the water for hours, and when I came out I sat at the tavern and ate fresh fish and drank. Snorkeling there was so wonderful because the sea was shallow and it formed an oxbow around Tolon and Drepanon, which made it perfect for snorkeling. I found certain Greek customs difficult to understand, like why they smashed clay plates on the floor during a communal dance where the men and women join arms and dance. Nevertheless, I felt a kinship with my Greek friends. They lived every day as if it were harvest time in the village.

While I was in Greece, Gaby and I decided to visit Istanbul, Turkey. I was quite reluctant to leave Greece, as I knew my Greek visa had expired. I was safe enough in the village of Assini, as I patiently waited for Tom to come rescue me from Greece. I hesitated at the idea of attempting to enter another country, but in the end, I was willing to take a chance and go to Turkey with the hope of safely returning back to Greece. Luckily, I was able to obtain the Turkish visa with no difficulty.

In Istanbul, Gaby and I visited the Swing Bridge over the Bosporus, which separates the East from the West over the two cities of Istanbul. We ate breakfast and dinner in the Pudding Shop, a tourist mecca and the exact location where the American Billy Hayes bought the drugs that landed him in prison in Turkey, a story portrayed in the movie *Midnight Express*. I tried to enjoy Istanbul but I was living in my head. I was quite concerned about whether I would be allowed back into Greece on an expired visa. What on earth would I do if they didn't let me back into the country? Did I have enough money to make it back to Italy?

We traveled back to Greece by very crowded train. Upon entering Greece, the customs officials came aboard checking passports. My heart was pounding the whole time. Would my expired visa be noticed? The customs official approached me and I handed him my passport. He opened a page and quickly glanced at it and handed it back to me and moved on. I kept worrying that he had noticed the expired visa, and that at the end of the trip he was going to come back for me. I didn't stop worrying until we reached Athens, and then I breathed a sigh of relief and thanked God for looking over me.

I was mostly angry at myself for having taken such a foolish and stupid risk. What if I had been refused re-entry into Greece? My plan to go to the US would have been jeopardized, if not ruined. What if I were deported back to Sierra Leone? That was now my biggest fear. For her part of my visa worries, Gaby apologized and assured me that she would have stood with me through whatever happened. I believed her. I returned to Assini and vowed not to leave Greece again until I heard from Tom.

Although Gaby and I were quite fond of each other, we both realized that our ultimate futures included a parting of the ways. Our relationship ended with her decision to go on to Australia. It was quite an emotional parting because we were very close.

Throughout my time in Greece I had remained in contact with the Stanganelli family in Gioia Tauro. I often telephoned them, and each time Anna Maria told me that they wanted me to come back to the Park Hotel. It made me feel good that the family missed me and wanted me back. I appreciated feeling like I had a safety net, a family I could always go back to in Italy. For the moment I felt safe in Assini on the expired Greek visa.

In essence, though, I was now stranded in Greece, and if I decided to return to Italy I had another problem: my Italian visa was now long expired. Challenging and difficult thoughts about my location in the world constantly occupied my mind. Should I take a chance and try to enter Italy on an expired visa? Or should I apply for another visa in Athens? What would be my chances of getting another Italian visa without Stefano or Tom's assistance? These problems plagued my mind. I knew there had to be a solution, but it didn't seem to be coming anytime soon.

Chapter 12

GABY HAD LEFT for Australia and the days seemed to pass by more slowly in her absence. I hadn't realized how much her excitement for everything kept me going. I sat down to write her and drew a blank. Even though I knew it was time for us to move on, I could not help missing my friend. That period in my life was marred by my separation from family and friends. I missed my mother, sisters, nieces, village people, Tom, baby Tara, the Stanganelli family, and now Gaby, and no amount of practice being apart from loved ones soothed the pain of parting. I pushed my thoughts to the plan that was in place. I only had to stick to the plan. Tom's challenge to me was that I be on my own for two years. The time had come to revisit the conversation about him sponsoring me to go to school in the U.S. I went on replacing thoughts of Gaby with fantasies about the US, and thinking about school helped ease my heartache. I was finally able to write the first of what would be several letters to her. Gaby and I maintained contact while she travelled in Australia and long after I had arrived and settled in the United States.

I kept hoping to hear from Tom, but I didn't have an address where he could reach me. The post office in Greece maintained what was called Post Restante at the front counter. Letters came for those with no address, and people could go there daily and look for any mail that may have arrived in their names. I had written to Tom through his parents' address in the United States and told him that I was with Gaby in Assini, Greece. I gave the Post Restante as my return address.

In 1983, Tom was the chief helicopter pilot flying for the American Evergreen Helicopters, based in McMinnville, Oregon. The company had a contract with Chevron Oil Company to conduct oil exploration in the African nation of Sudan. I knew that his career would mostly keep him spending his time in Africa. I wondered about how baby Tara was growing; she would soon be school aged. Thinking about baby Tara helped me take the focus off of how badly I wanted to hear from Tom.

I had decided to send Tom another telegram asking him directly how we would reunite, but before I could send it, much to my delight I received wonderful news. One of my friend's girlfriends informed me that there was a postcard waiting for me at the post office. I left the café, running in the direction of the post office. I hoped upon hope that it would be from Tom, and it was. His postcard read, "Dear Francis. I arrived in Nafplio, Greece, and I am staying in the hotel at the pier."

I was overjoyed. I read the postcard over and over again. My big dream might finally be coming true. I had always looked at my time in Greece as something I simply needed to endure. My makeshift plan with Tom, to talk about America in two years, had been enough to keep me in the fields under the hot Mediterranean sun. I pictured Tom rescuing me from the hard labor of Greece. Of course I still liked it in Assini; I had friends, I had work. Everything was there, yet not enough to ease my yearning for an education in the United States.

I immediately went to the hotel in Nafplio, which was about seven miles away. On the bus ride my mind was churning and my palms were sweaty. I studied the face of the postcard and could not find the postmark date showing when Tom had mailed it. I became extremely concerned that maybe Tom had spent days waiting for me and I worried that he had already left. These thoughts made my stomach turn flips. What would I do if I had missed him?

When I got to the hotel and gave Tom's name, the receptionist smiled and said, "The American? Yes, he is here." I was so relieved. She rang his room while I waited. I watched as he descended the stairs, and my excitement seemed to ramp up with his every step. I hadn't seen him since 1980, and more than two years of excitement was bubbling over inside of me. Just as he took the final step down, I had the strangest thought. What if Tom had come just to check and see how I was living, inspecting my home like he did when I lived with my cousin Alfred at Gaia Camp. I hoped that he had come all this way for more than just a visit. He was my model for honesty and loyalty, and he was my best hope to get to the United States.

I pushed these thoughts out of my mind as Tom and I shook hands and embraced. We went outside to the veranda overlooking the port and the server appeared instantly and took our orders for beers. I waited for Tom to begin the conversation; I was afraid of saying the wrong thing. The only thing on my mind was going to America. My heart was racing. Did he come to tell me he couldn't afford to send me to America? Maybe he had an alternate plan for me, I thought as he lit a cigarette. Tom commented on the weather, and from there our conversation drifted to old acquaintances as we sipped our cold beers. Before long we were both relaxed, and Tom was wearing a bright smile. He seemed genuinely happy to see me. He must have wondered how I had done it all. I hoped that he would be proud of me. I listened intently to his words during that visit.

He said, "Francis, I am very proud of you. You came to Europe on your own, and through the Sahara. How did you make it? How were the Stanganellis?" Before I could answer any of his questions, he opened the floodgates saying, "Have you applied to any schools in America?" There it was! Finally, I heard what I had hoped for. I thought *I am finally going to America.* I told him I had met an American whose father had sent me information about Springfield Technical Community College. Tuition was about $1,200 per year. Tom looked at me and said, "Well, you want to go to America for school, and I will pay for your school and your board." I was stunned by his generosity.

"Tom, words can't express how happy I am right now, thank you. And to think I may finally get to meet your parents. Your mother has been …" I stopped talking because Tom began to hold his head in his hands. I reached out and touched his shoulder. "What is it, Tom," I whispered.

"I'm afraid you will not get to meet my dad. He died from a heart attack," Tom said with his voice cracking. I inquired about his mother, and he assured me she was OK. He continued to wear a look of distress on his face.

"Something else is on your mind, my friend," I said in the lightest tone I could manage. Tom told me that he had broken up with Shauana, and that she had returned to Colorado Springs and taken baby Tara with her. I felt for him. Here I was celebrating my good fortune with him once again, and he had nothing but sad news to share. When I asked him about what happened between him and Shauana he rolled his eyes and said, "You wouldn't understand."

The way he clammed up at my question reminded me of my other unanswered question: why had he left Sierra Leone so abruptly? I never had the chance to ask him about it in Tamale, but I assumed that he would, in fact, tell me this time around. Now that I felt he had gained confidence in me, now that I felt I had proven myself to him, I figured he would tell me why he had deserted me in Sierra Leone in 1976. I sensed that this was not the right moment to broach the subject, so I decided to let our conversation unfold organically.

I told Tom that I had a farm house in Assini, which a Greek farmer let me live in for free. Tom agreed to check out of the hotel and come to the farm house to bunk in one of the rooms there. He settled in easily, and I introduced him to all my European friends who were, of course, hanging around the farm house night and day. Tom was on vacation for one month, and he said his work schedule would easily allow him to come back to see me again. Thank God. I was lucky about this development, as it meant Tom could return to help me get my visa to America.

One afternoon in Tolon, Tom and I sat down at a tavern overlooking the Mediterranean. I was always thanking him for his generosity and for his kindness. I felt Tom and I had grown closer during this time together, so I opened up to him about Alfred's maltreatment of me. I appreciated his life advice: "Francis, you must learn to forgive." However, I didn't even understand the concept of forgiveness, nor how to go about it, until much later in life. At any rate, his advice took root in my heart. Tom stopped looking at the water to direct his gaze at me. He wore a serious look on his face and pursed his lips for a long moment before continuing.

He finally asked me, "Francis, how was your travel, especially through the Sahara. I was at times concerned. How did you make it?" I knew he would ask me about my dangerous journey through the mighty Sahara, and I was prepared to narrate. I chronicled every detail of my trials and tribulations in the desert, including the near death incident, how I was smuggled into Algeria, and again at the Tunisian border. I could sense he was truly amazed at how I had made it on my own. I'm sure Tom wondered why I had never reached out to him when I was having a hard time, especially after I nearly died. I had my explanation of how I wanted to make it on my own, but he never asked.

Sitting on the veranda, watching the water and sipping our drinks, I felt that the moment had arrived. We were sharing all sorts of things about our lives, and I still desperately needed to know why he had left Sierra Leone so abruptly. I knew he didn't leave to get away from me, but I still felt abandoned. I eased the question in after our third round of drinks.

Tom burst out laughing. "Francis, there was this guy whose name I can't recall now, but he was the Chief of Police in Sierra Leone. He was appointed head of all the police forces of Sierra Leone by the president. I often flew this guy and other high ranking officials to check on mining operations."

I began to rack my brain trying to recall the name of the man who was Chief of Police when Tom was in Sierra Leone in 1976. Then suddenly I blurted out the man's name and Tom immediately snapped his fingers and said, "Yes, that's him! I recall that name from my flight logs from Sierra Leone in 1976."

I interrupted Tom and said, "He was an important politician and Chief of Police of Sierra Leone. He was also the government-appointed Chief of Security in the diamond mines in the Kono District and everybody was afraid of him."

Tom told me he'd flown this man many times. He said, "I didn't speak to him when I flew him to the mines because I sensed he was an arrogant man, and there was something weird about him. He must have thought I snubbed him. One night I was at the bar with my friend Dennis McFadden, you remember McFadden, the Irish guy I often played poker with. We were complaining about work-related issues. I had said that for weeks the stupid government in Freetown had been holding parts for the helicopters at the port. The engineers had wanted the parts to work on the helicopters. That was all I said. Evidently we were overheard discussing this, because all of a sudden a guy appeared in my face and said "I am the Chief of Police of Sierra Leone, you are under arrest for speaking against the government."

Tom said this caused a great commotion at the bar. He said, "I was taken to the Motema police station in a Land Rover by two of his officers. I sat in the station all night long. In the morning R.C. Sturgeon, the General Manager of NDMC, came down in his new Mercedes and told me that under orders of the government of Sierra Leone I had to leave the country within 24 hours. It had already been arranged that I would fly to Freetown, then to London and then home to America.

"As I sat in Sturgeon's office my friends Dennis McFadden and Peter Gregory came to see what had happened. Dennis rolled his eyes in contempt, and called Jalloh a bloody wanker. I had to let you know so I came to the school. I'm sorry it was so hard for you, Francis, to have me leave after only a couple of months.

"In London I walked into Autair International, the company I was working for in Sierra Leone, and the president apologized for what had happened. The next day I flew to Minneapolis. My mother picked me up from the airport, and I was home. I told Mom and Dad what had happened, and I told them about you, too. I told them I had met an African boy that I had volunteered to help with his education. My parents were so proud of me for taking up such a noble and moral cause."

Tom told me he hadn't liked working in the diamond industry because of the injustices, the political corruption, and the economic deprivation of the people of the country. "After all," he said, "your people owned the land and therefore the diamonds, and yet they live in abject poverty. Do you remember the Separator House where I met your cousin?"

I nodded my head. "Yes. Yes I do."

"Every day diamonds were brought from the mines into that Separator House. There were millions and millions of dollars' worth of diamonds coming out of the Kono District alone every day, yet the people who lived there were extremely poor. At least twice every month a pilot would land on the roof of the Separator House and transport boxes of diamonds to Freetown."

I interrupted, saying, "Yes, yes. I often saw the helicopters land on top of the Separator House."

Tom continued, saying, "Listen, at least twice every month I would land on top of that Separator house, and either Dennis or Dave Walker would come up with sizeable boxes that contained finished, packaged diamonds. They were loaded onto the helicopter and an officer would handcuff himself to the box—an idea I thought was rather stupid. I then flew them to Lungi International at Freetown, where a British Airways jet would be waiting to take the diamonds to London.

"Another reason I didn't like working for NDMC was that your people were prohibited from digging for diamonds on your very own land. One of the operations of the pilots was to go after the 'illicit' diamond miners. Now, who were these people?" he asked. "I suspect it was your own people. Your people were not illicit people. They should be able to dig for diamonds on their own land." He gazed at me and said, "I'm sorry you felt bad when I left, but honestly, I was happy to leave Sierra Leone."

He went on, "I was happy to work for Viking Helicopters in Ghana. On that job I was helping people by treating the rivers in order to kill the tsetse flies that caused people to go blind. It made me feel good about myself that I was not helping exploit people but making a difference in their lives, helping my fellow man rather than making them miserable."

I listened attentively. I could tell Tom was quite passionate about the topic. This conversation renewed my faith in him as a good, compassionate man. I chuckled internally at the idea that I ever suspected Tom of diamond theft. Tom told me he'd first come to Africa in 1974 to do crop dusting in Mali, Ghana, Nigeria, Rwanda, Uganda and Burundi for a British company called Autair International. He had also worked in the UK doing crop dusting. He told me he worked in England, Scotland, Ireland and northern Switzerland. I marveled over all the places that Tom's work had taken him. He essentially traveled for a living. I listened in amazement at his stories.

Tom said, "Francis, I've flown over every town and village in the Kono District. There were three operating mining plants that ran day and night."

I interrupted him, saying, "Yes I know, and I know the names of all three operating diamond mining plants, Numbers 11, 12, and 7. I passed by one, I think it was Number 12, on the way to the town of Jaiama Nimikoro. I often saw the heavy-duty machines digging up the gravel. I watched the diamond trucks entering the Separator House. As a boy I vividly remember seeing this—"

Tom interrupted me and said, "Stop right there. Listen, I was one of the pilots who provided air cover for the convoys traveling from the processing plants carrying the fine sediments containing the diamonds to the Separator House. As the convoy traveled from the mines to the Separator House, pilots would provide air cover. There were also two heavily armed security escort vehicles, one in front of the convoy and one in the back. The mining plants were located in dense areas up to 20 miles from the Separator House. What I saw with my own eyes was blatant exploitation of your people and your country. It seemed pretty outrageous to me. NDMC was extracting enough wealth to build and maintain roads throughout your country. I don't understand how your politicians could have been so neglectful of your people."

Tom shook his head and paused, awaiting my response. Tom knew quite a lot about the diamond operations in my country. I knew he could not have stolen diamonds, and I did not tell him that that's why I thought he'd left so abruptly. I knew my country was endowed with natural resources such as diamonds, iron, gold, piassava, bauxite and agricultural products such as coffee, cacao, palm oil, yet none of the proceeds from these natural resources have been used to benefit the people of Sierra Leone.

The next conversation we had was more specific to me personally and centered on my plans to go to America to attend college. As we sat on the porch of my farm house in Assini, I told Tom my many concerns and apprehensions. My visas for both Italy and Greece had expired. What were my chances of getting an American student visa in Greece? Tom and I both agreed that I should return to Italy and stay with the Stanganellis and apply for the American visa there. The Stanganellis were people of substance and could be helpful as a reference when dealing with the American consulate. The back-up plan, in case I was not issued a visa in Italy, was to return home to Sierra Leone and apply for the American student visa from there.

Tom promised that he would write to his mother and ask her to pay my first semester's tuition at Springfield Technical Community College. She would send the receipt of the payment to Tom, and he would bring it with him the next time he came to see me. Making plans to actually go to America was a surreal experience. For years I had turned over thoughts about living in the US in my thoughts, and now the thoughts were coming to life.

Throughout Tom's stay with me in Assini, he repeatedly told me how proud he was of me, and that he was pleased to help me with my education. On each occasion I met with Tom I took the opportunity to thank him over and over. I was concerned about the costs of an airplane ticket back to Sierra Leone, and then more airfare for me to travel to the United States, in addition to the costs and expenses he was willing to incur for my tuition, room and board in America. I prayed, *God, I know that you don't make dreams come half true. I trust that you will make a way for me, yet again. Thank you for my friend Tom.*

Tom had to return to Sudan, and he and I arranged that he would return in three months. At that time he would come to Italy to see me and the Stanganelli family at the Park Hotel. I travelled with Tom to Athens, at which point we separated: he went on to Sudan while I returned to Assini to prepare for my trip back to Italy.

I telephoned the Stanganellis and told Anna I was returning to the Park Hotel. She quickly replied, "Ba bene. Si bene ca pronto," so I knew I was welcome. I would miss Assini. I had gotten quite comfortable there, and I would miss my friends. But I was thankful that I was leaving the country under fortunate circumstances, especially compared to being deported for having an expired visa. Still, my heart ached at the idea that I would probably never see most of my friends in Assini again. The connections I had formed in Greece were not easily severed. I went around to the taverns and farms saying my goodbyes.

After an uneventful flight, I arrived at the Park Hotel to the Stanganellis' open arms. I wasted no time telling them of my plans of going to America. Anna was confused at this statement. She looked at me as if asking, "Help you go to America?"

Yes, I had some explaining to do.

Chapter 13

ON A TUESDAY morning in May, I answered Peppino's call to me in the kitchen. I emerged drying my hands on my apron and was completely surprised to see Tom standing there. I had spoken to the family often about Tom, and they knew that he was a friend of Stefano's. Still, I noticed the family staring at Tom with great curiosity. I imagined they wondered why this blond-haired man had traveled all the way to meet with me in Italy. The family knew Tom was a helicopter pilot, but they did not know the details of our connection. When I'd told the Stanganellis about America, I had not explained the details of the circumstances in which I had met Tom.

Tom made small talk with Peppino and Anna Maria, and the afternoon passed pleasantly, if awkwardly so. Two days later, May 25, 1984, came the day of reckoning for me. On this day, Tom and I visited the US consulate in Palermo, Sicily, and I applied for an F-1 student visa, without which I wouldn't be able to enter the United States. I'd worked hard while in Greece and had acquired all the necessary immigration documents for the FI visa to attend Springfield Technical Community College. The school had already issued me Form I-20 affirming that my first semester's tuition had been paid. I also had an affidavit of support commitment agreement from Tom stating that he would be financially supporting me in the United States. Tom sensed my apprehension about my expired visa and said, "Let's wait and see. Stop worrying. Let's see what happens."

With my documents in hand and Tom behind me, I walked up to the glass window. I could see an American flag hoisted on a golden stand, and on the wall was the picture of then US President Ronald Reagan next to a picture of then US Secretary of State George Schultz. The American officials dressed in colorful uniforms. Tom later told me the officials were members of the United States Marines.

As I approached the counter a man rose to help me. I spoke to him saying, "I have been accepted to attend college at the Springfield Technical Community College in Springfield, Massachusetts. I am here with my sponsor Tom Johnson to apply for a visa to attend school in the United States."

The official took all of my documents, including my passport, and looked at Tom standing behind me. He walked away with my documents and went into the adjacent room so Tom and I went back and sat down. The wait was unbearable. I twisted in my seat and rearranged the pamphlets that were sitting on the table. I saw several Italian families with their children in the waiting room. I was sure they were also applying for visas to immigrate to the United States. I watched the kids rolling all over the thick blue carpet. Tom and I said nothing to each other while we waited. He watched with a half smirk as I fidgeted. Our eyes met repeatedly, but we just sat in silence with our eyes fixated on the room where the officer went with my papers.

After what felt like an eternity, but was probably about ten minutes, we saw the officer come out from the office. He had my papers and my passport in his hand as he returned to the counter. Tom and I rose to meet him at the counter. The officer gave me all of my papers and my passport back and said, "You will have to apply for the visa in your home country of Sierra Leone." My heart dropped to the pit of my stomach. I was not just disappointed, I felt that my entire world had just shattered. The shock was palpable. Tom and I stood at the counter with blank stares. Tom had taken time and had traveled all the way from Sudan to Italy to help me obtain my visa. I had all the necessary documents and Tom had generously volunteered to incur the financial expenses for my move to the United States only to be refused a visa because I was in a foreign country. I was dumbfounded.

Suddenly the same officer came back to the counter and asked me to return my documents. I pushed them under the glass back and Tom and I continued to stand in silence. We were both baffled with wonder and hope. We went and sat down. Our eyes were now fixated on the official's every move. With my documents in his hand I saw him return to the back office, and after a while he came out. My heart was pounding, my palms were sweating, and my eyes were glued on his every move. I saw him come from the office, this time holding only my passport in his hand. I watched as he turned the pages and placed my passport under what looked like a stamping device. We watched as he pulled a lever, imprinting my passport. I had not uttered a single word the entire time, instead silently praying to God for his assistance. When I saw the officer stamp my passport, I leaned over to Tom and said, "I think I got the visa."

He replied, "I'll believe it when I see it."

The officer examined a page in my passport carefully and then wrote something in it. Finally he approached the counter, holding my passport in his hand, beckoning me forward. He said, "The cost of the visa is $25."

My body relaxed in one great heave. I knew that Jesus and the Holy Ghost were guiding my fate. I had been prepared to accept and endure whatever happened, but I kept hope alive. I knew that God had bestowed His grace upon me yet again. I have no idea why he came back, why I got the visa, but I was too happy to ask.

Tom and I were jubilant. The officer handed Tom his change and me my passport then said to me, "Welcome to the United States." Tom and I shook hands while we walked down the stairs on the soft carpet. We just kept on shaking hands and smiling at each other. We also kept looking at the visa like it was a magical thing. Then we took the bus to the train station, and I sang and whistled the whole time. I said hello to everyone I passed. Tom and I went to a café for lunch before taking the train from Palermo to Gioia Tauro, via Messina. We were on the ferry boat across the Straits when Tom finally said, "Francis, you are one lucky guy." Tears of joy and gratitude overwhelmed me. I had no answer for the miraculous event at the US consulate aside from God.

In my heart and mind I wondered what motivated Tom. He could have cut me off at any time, but he did not—he kept his promises. He had taught me what real friendship was. I had never been so happy in my life.

I wore a huge smile when we arrived at the Park Hotel, and the whole family knew something good had happened to me. I told the Stanganelli family that I had received a visa to go to America. They were happy, but I could still see that they were puzzled. I imagined they were wondering about the motives behind Tom's support of me too.

That happy evening Peppe, the oldest son of Peppino who had been away at medical school in Messina, came home. He brought a friend who was studying at MIT in Boston, whom he had mentioned whenever I talked about my plans to go to America. Peppe said that he too would very much like to go to America. In fact, I sensed that everyone in the family wanted to go to America. When he heard I had my visa he looked at me in admiration: all Italians knew that it was hard to get an American visa.

Anna Maria had prepared a special spaghetti dish, including calamari, in Tom's honor, but Tom had to hurry to catch his train for Rome the same evening. He was returning to Sudan, back to flying for Evergreen Helicopters on an oil exploration contract from Chevron Oil Company. Tom and I went up to my room where Tom gave me $700 US dollars. He also gave me a $5,000 check postdated for September 14th. He told me to immediately buy an airline ticket and to be wise with the rest of the money until school started.

Tony drove Tom and me to the train station, less than a mile away, and I stayed with Tom while he waited for the train. I could tell he was exhausted. As we waited alone in the train station I kept thanking Tom for his generosity. He told me, "Francis, stop thanking me. This is what you've always wanted, and I am delighted to be helping you. America is a big country with all kinds of different people. Be careful. There are many attractions, but stay focused on school. I am sure the school will help you find temporary lodging until you find a place. Massachusetts is a good place for education, but it's an expensive place to live. Your first school semester is paid and I will send the second semester tuition when you need it. It's very cold in Massachusetts, like my home state of Minnesota, so you will need warm clothes. You have my mother's telephone in the States and you can always talk to her."

I never forgot these words. Tom's friendship meant more than financial security. I had joined his family. I wondered what my mother would think of Tom. I thought about all the chances I'd had to take him to my village to meet her. I thought about how, without Tom, a fatherless boy like me would have had to live out my days impoverished and miserable in Sierra Leone. Here was God, sending me a brother, father and a friend.

We heard the approaching train and knew that it was time for us to part. It was an emotional farewell. The next time I would see him would be at my graduation from college in Springfield, Massachusetts in 1986.

Back at the Park Hotel I had to make plans. I wondered how I could ever pay Tom back. My travel plans endowed me with a new stature at the hotel. The family, employees and guests all openly admired me because of my plans to go to America.

I still had three months before I started school, and I have to admit I was very worried about my money. I concealed my passport and money in my mattress in my room. I did not leave the hotel very often, as I worried about the safety of my money. If I lost it, I would be ruined. I trusted the family, but I lived in a hotel where guests came and went. Anna Maria noted my angst, and when I told her my worry she took my valuables and placed them in the safe.

I was excited and eager to see America, but I hadn't been in school since 1980. The thought of a college education was somewhat intimidating. I thought of all the students I had met on vacation from their studies. I thought it might be a good idea to go see some of those friends I'd made throughout my travels in Greece and Italy, so I decided to spend my time until school started visiting friends all over Europe.

I said a bittersweet "Ciao, ciao" to my family, and Tony drove me to the train station to catch my train. The next day I arrived in Rome early in the morning. I found a cheap youth hostel and bought a standby ticket on British Airways, one way to Boston. I went to the British consulate and applied for a transit visa. For the first time I was not nervous in a consulate, wondering whether or not I would get a visa. In fact, I was confident I would be given a visa to visit England. I collected the British and French visas I needed without event. It was incredibly empowering to operate independently and acquire my travel papers.

In a matter of weeks I visited Rome, the Vatican, the Sistine Chapel, the masterpiece by Michelangelo, and St. Peter's Square. I crossed yet another famous body of water, the ancient Tiber River. The youth hostel in

Turino lay in a quiet, wooded estate. An old Italian lady tended to the hostel. She dressed in layers: some sort of outwear apparel over the top of what appeared to be a uniform. I remember how quaint and extremely clean the lodging was, and how friendly the innkeeper had been. She prepared breakfast every morning.

I stopped in several cities on my way to Paris. My friend Marquez was glad to see me. He asked, "You are going to America, Francois?"

I answered, "Oui, je vais à l'Amérique." I had to respond in French as I was in a jubilant mood. I showed him my visa and explained everything to him. Paris was my first time experiencing the underground transit system—yes, I rode the legendary French subway, visited the Eiffel Tower, the Notre Dame Cathedral, and the Place de la Bastille. I couldn't comprehend how a train could travel underneath the earth, and even under water. While riding the train I contemplated how God made the universe. At what point did God expect man to split the English Channel? God was indeed miraculous; He is the creator of the waterway and the person who figured out how to split it. God made history and put me in contact with it. I thought back to my history lessons on the French Revolution at school in Sierra Leone. Standing in the square of Place de la Bastille that was once a prison, I felt surrounded by stories of the many prisoners who lost their lives. God was responsible for my adventures. As a matter of fact, my whole life belonged to God, because God had used the couple in Tessalit to save my life. I rode along on the train thanking God for all my trials, tribulations and victories.

After a week in Paris I left for my next stop in Folkestone, England to see Derrick. Back home in Sierra Leone, a British crown colony, our image of England was large and mystical. To get to the English Channel, I took the underground and the bus to Calais where I then took the hovercraft across the English Channel to Folkestone. I was startled by the hovercraft; it looked like an airplane, but it also looked like a boat. The pontoons beneath it were deflated as people boarded the vessel. It was typical English weather, cloudy and misty. When we were loaded I saw the propellers turning and heard the roar of the engines.

Standing on British soil for the first time was an emotional experience. Most of my school teachers were British and I had heard a lot about

England. Many people in my country yearned to come to England one day. Of course, for me, America held the ultimate appeal, and soon I would be crossing the Atlantic Ocean to America. I was excited to see new parts of the world, with new and colorful people and cultures, and wished I was already at my final destination and settled down. I longed for normalcy. Derrick told me that Greg and Lorna, my best friends in Assini, lived nearby in a town called Walmer so I decided to visit them, too. They were not as surprised as Derrick when I came to visit them. They had met Tom in Assini; in fact, Tom and another friend named Terry McGuire and his girlfriend, Hiker, spent several days on the beach in Drepanon, and it was Hiker who got me Tom's postcard from the post office.

Next stop London.

In the London's Piccadilly Square I saw a lady selling fish and chips. I asked how much and she said, "One quid and half." I was bewildered as I stood in line trying to figure out what she meant. I had just exchanged $100 US dollars for English silver, and there had been no mention of quid. I watched her wrap the fish and chips in newspaper and hand them to her customers. I waited until she was not so busy to ask her. "One and a half British pounds," she said. I bought a soft drink and sat to eat lunch and people watched.

After my meal I left the square in search for the hostel. I asked a police officer for directions to Hammersmith. He spoke with a thick accent and he was trying to be helpful, but I did not understand a word he was saying. Thankfully a lady overheard our conversation and stepped in and told the officer that she would show me the correct underground train to take. She advised me that the officer was from Scotland, and that "those Scots have their own way of talking."

When I got to Hammersmith, I asked for directions to Tent City, which is a cheap open space facility where, for a minimum fee, you can put up your tent and stay. They also had cheap rooms and basic facilities. It catered to adventurers and vagabonds, many from America. The place reminded me of Assini in atmosphere and diversity—all that was missing was the beach. Here I was, actually in London. I humbly thanked God for Tom's generosity and once again wondered why the Lord had blessed me with all this.

The next day I was the last passenger to board the British Airways flight bound for Logan International Airport in Boston. Luckily I got a window seat and caught my last glimpses of London out the window. I was as ambivalent as ever. On the one hand my dream was coming true, but on the other I worried about the uncertainty that lay ahead. I kept thanking God for blessing me with a friend like Tom.

The aircraft began its roll down the runway. There was an increase in engine roar, and then we were moving fast. I felt a slight sinking sensation in my stomach, and I looked out the window to see England dropping lower and lower, everything getting smaller and smaller. Soon all I could see was a big blur. I realized we were over the mighty Atlantic Ocean.

The flight lasted about six hours, and throughout I kept thinking of not only the big picture of my future, but also my more immediate concerns. How was I going to get from Boston to Springfield, Massachusetts? Where was I going to sleep that night? My mind wandered from logistics to anxieties over cultural differences. Would Americans be kind like Tom, and friendly like Matthew? My conversations with Tom in Gioia Tauro came back to me, as did all of Tom's advice.

My thoughts went all the way back to school in Sierra Leone where I learned that a great American president, John F. Kennedy was born in Boston and later sadly assassinated in Dallas, Texas. Back in Sierra Leone, President Kennedy's school meal program furnished my primary school with a steady flow of wheat, corn meal, corn oil, butter, and powdered milk from America. We were reminded that it was America's President John Kennedy who was responsible. In my case the American food I ate at school was often the only food I ate on the many days my cousin starved me.

As we prepared to land, my thoughts returned to the present. With a little squeak of rubber on asphalt, a quick thump and the roar of reverse thrusting jet engines, the plane finally landed at Boston's Logan Airport. My emotions soared. Happy, jubilant, grateful, hesitant, scared, they were all there.

At immigration I handed my passport to the female officer. She opened it and flipped the pages and found my American visa. She examined the visa and stamped on the adjacent pages, then handed the passport back to me. A new feeling, one of freedom flowed over me. I was cleared, and I was in America.

At the information booth I learned where I could get a bus to Springfield, and I was directed to the shuttle bus stop where a smaller bus would take me to the Peter Pan bus terminal, where I would then get on a bigger bus to Springfield.

My first impression of America was that everything looked gigantic. There were very big cars and roads wide enough to accommodate three cars going in the same direction at one time. The eighteen wheeler trucks were enormous. On the bus I rode past miles and miles of green landscape and then miles of houses. It was never ending.

Once I arrived at the Springfield bus station I asked for the location of the YMCA. A woman with a shaved head and a Boston accent pointed outside and told me, "You go straight up on Liberty Street. The Y is on Chestnut Street, two blocks from here."

I understood everything except what a block was. She gazed at me with wonder and then, realizing I was a foreigner, said, "You go two streets over, and you will see the YMCA sign up the street on Chestnut."

It was a ten-minute walk to the YMCA. On the way I saw a United States Post Office and people going in and coming out. I walked up Liberty Street, the home of several tall buildings. One in particular was a four story unit with big wide windows and a sign reading IBM. I marveled over the architecture, the traffic and the people. I think my entire village would have fit in the space between the bus station and the YMCA.

At the Y's reception desk I explained that I had just arrived in the country and that I was a student at STCC. A lady approached me from the office and said that she could help me. After I showed her my passport and documents she gave me a key to my room on the third floor overlooking Chestnut and Liberty Streets, without telling me the rent. In my room I let out a sigh of relief. I was tired and hungry, but content. And I was in America.

Chapter 14

AFTER I GOT settled in I went downstairs to the restaurant. I was not all familiar with an American menu. I saw a man eating what appeared to be two round pieces of bread with meat and tomatoes in the middle. I also noticed what looked to me like fried yams, but longer and thinner. I asked the waitress to explain the menu to me. She spoke fast and, though I tried hard to understand her English, I couldn't. She stood there looking at me expecting my order. I froze, embarrassed. I finally spoke and told her that I was new to America. She took a step back from the table and cradled her receipt book. She smiled and said, "No problem." I told her I would have what the gentleman beside me was having. She explained that it was a hamburger and french fries, in fact the menu consisted mostly of burgers.

It was awkward to pick up the burger. I grabbed it with both hands and examined it closely. The vibrancy of the red tomato made me think happy thoughts. I sniffed the burger and found the spices and the meat aromatic. I took one last look around the room and then fixated on the burger. I felt like I opened my mouth wider than it could physically expand and I sank my teeth into the layered delight in my hands. Let's just say that the American cheeseburger gave spaghetti a run for its money.

The next day I found out that it took two buses to get from the Y to STCC. I got on the bus and told the driver, "I am going to STCC on State Street. Please let me out there." I sat close to him so I could easily hear when he told me to get off. I stared out the window, trying to process all that I was seeing. I noted landmarks and the names of intersections. I saw a grocery store, a gas station, and a pet store. Eventually the bus stopped and the driver pointed to the left saying, "There is STCC."

The buildings were all brown brick. They appeared old, and I noticed that the school was in the middle of the city of Springfield. The STCC campus was fenced off with corrugated iron railings. Inside the administration building I asked for the Dean of Student's Office. The guard walked me to the end of the hallway where I met William Manzi, the Dean of Students. Mr. Manzi was very friendly. I showed him my documents and told him I had a check for five thousand dollars which my sponsor had postdated for me to deposit in the bank next month. The dean advised me not to hold onto the check but to deposit it right away, as he said the bank would hold it until it cleared. He said I could give the bank his name and number if they had any concerns.

Mr. Manzi introduced me to President Schebili, a tall, friendly man. He welcomed me to STCC and thanked me for choosing his school. The dean took me on a tour of the school campus, which was not that big. It consisted of several old buildings, and Mr. Manzi told me that the STCC campus was once an armory where guns were manufactured. He mentioned Smith and Wesson. Then the dean took me to the school cafeteria where I had my second burger with french fries.

STCC was a two-year community college, and I would major in General Studies. I was ready to begin, but I would have to wait a while longer, as it was still only early August.

I walked back to the bus stop thinking, *here I am in Springfield, Massachusetts, in a country I have always dreamed of, always thought of, always imagined, and a country I always prayed to go to.* I thanked God it was happening. Back at the Y, I telephoned Tom's mother Virginia and told her that I had arrived in Springfield and that I'd met with the Dean of Students at the school, and that I was temporarily staying at the Y. She told me that Tom was still flying in Khartoum, in the Sudan. I told her that I had not experienced the culture shock that I had expected, probably because I had already been to Europe and had been exposed to Europeans. I felt like my interactions with Europeans had prepared me to deal with American people, which was not to say that I knew anything about America. I knew of no Africans in Springfield that I could have related to or relied on to show me around or to orient me to the environment. She assured me that she was behind me and so was Tom. It felt good to know that the Johnsons were in my corner. Of course, I was a survivor and I had trust in my own resourcefulness and in God.

I found my way around by walking the streets and learning the bus routes. I discovered that the black population was concentrated on the north side in an area called Winchester Square. I walked along Boston Road going toward the north side and stopped into a library in the Winchester Square neighborhood. I told the librarian that I had just arrived in the US and I was looking for a room to rent. She directed me to the building across the street.

The red brick building had a sign that read Urban League of Springfield on the front, and I noted considerable pedestrian traffic in front of the building. I crossed the street and entered. I told the receptionist that I was new to this country, and that I was a student and needed a home to rent while attending school. She was a very light-skinned, older African American woman. She was quite interested to know that I was from Africa and asked what country I was from. Suddenly she started to comment on how unjust it was to keep Nelson Mandela in prison, and she seemed more interested in African politics than my particular problem. She went on and on about colonialism and other injustices perpetrated against the African people. I couldn't even pretend to feign interest.

When she realized that I wasn't interested in her conversation, she said, "I have a room you can rent in my home." I hesitated to respond. She said, "You can live in my home. My daughter got married and left the house. The upstairs room is available. It has a kitchen, too." Here again I felt truly blessed with God's grace. She said her name was Corinthia Williams, and she gave me her home address and phone number. I told her I was currently staying at the Y and school started next month. She said, "Come by and meet my husband." Then she added, "Wait, my husband and I will come by the Y and pick you up on Sunday afternoon."

That Sunday I was standing outside the Y when they pulled up. Her husband was a very nice, religious man. Their home was in the Winchester neighborhood of Springfield. She had prepared a meal for me of fried chicken, mashed potatoes and gravy, and green peas. I could sense that Mrs.

Williams was thrilled about me just arriving from Africa. I had not yet told her that I'd spent some time in Europe.

After dinner she showed me the room. It was an upstairs apartment in a single family home. The bedroom already had a bed in the room, and Mrs. Williams said she could give me sheets. The floors were finished oak with a small bathroom and living room. The kitchen was located downstairs. She asked me what I could afford to pay, and I racked my brain for a number. I had done some research about rent in the area. My problem was that I didn't know what was referred to as an apartment. In England I'd heard Derrick refer to his place as a flat. So while I had a general idea, I wasn't sure. I told her I could afford $300 a month. Mr. Williams said that would be fine with them if I could pay my own electric cost. Again, a subject I knew nothing about. I didn't tell them that, though, and I agreed to pay for the electric. I asked if I could move in sooner than the end of the month. I had already registered for school and would attend classes Monday through Friday from 9am to 2pm. The Williams were quite amenable and generous to me, allowing me to move in right away and giving me a bed and some furniture.

Meanwhile, I had already met some new friends at the Y, three European exchange students, one from Sweden and two from Scotland. We traded travel stories and enjoyed many laughs. As much as I was beginning to settle in, I was also beginning to feel some stress. I hadn't been in school since 1980, and I feared failing my courses. I was undecided which career to pursue at the time, although I was interested in telecommunications. The uncertainties in my life were threatening to steal my joy. I prayed often, asking God to reveal his plan to me. I could see myself graduating with Tom in the front row. I imagined that by some miracle my mother would be sitting in the front row, too.

In the fall, cold winds began to blow just like Tom told me they would. Living in constant inclement weather was quite a jolt for me. I immediately bought boots, gloves and two overcoats. Try as I might, I couldn't get used to the cold. I even stayed in my room one day because it was just too cold to go outside.

One day I was in the library when two of my classmates, Grahame Pearson and Robert Ganest, told me that they would pick me up at my place at about 6:00 that evening. They were taking me to a function, but I had no clue as to what the function was. Shortly after 6:00 we drove to Ganest's house. Nicholas and three other students from STCC were there. It was getting dark and we all piled into Robert's car and drove to a farmhouse owned by one of the student's parents. I was shocked to see horses outside the stable.

I asked Grahame, "Why are we here?"

"We are going on a hayride," he said.

"What is that?"

"It's Halloween, and a hayride is a custom here."

Everyone was rolling around in the hay and I found the jubilant mood hard to understand. Here we were in the cold, about to ride around on a horse-drawn wagon in the dark. I decided to be a good sport about it because I did not want to miss out on a new experience. I got on board the cart and off we went into the dark forests of Springfield.

Our first stop was in a graveyard. I was upset. I had never done anything so strange. My friends were just the opposite, happy and excited. Finally, a friend explained the custom and tradition of Halloween. He told me about the witches of Salem, and how the tradition of Halloween started in America. He explained that everybody looks forward to Halloween, and the kids dress up in scary costumes and go from house to house hunting for candy. It made little sense to me. I had learned about witchcraft in my home country of Sierra Leone. I knew that voodoo was evil and bad. Therefore, I was wondering why the Americans were celebrating something evil like voodoo. I asked if the white people had witchcraft too, as I was quite aware of the superstitions surrounding it in Africa. It was about this time that I also learned of another beloved American tradition, Thanksgiving.

I came to take this holiday quite personally and have incorporated it into my own life. I celebrated my first Thanksgiving with the Williams family that November. I could sense that Thanksgiving was a big and very important holiday in America, since everything was closed. I was told that Thanksgiving was, just as the name implied, about people giving thanks and being grateful for what they had. I quickly picked up on the idea and became thankful myself, making the entire concept an important part of my life. I felt so grateful to be in America, with good friends and so much opportunity. Most of all, I was thankful to God for how gracious He had been to me. God had watched over me in ways that I could never even have imagined, and those were just the blessings I knew about. After the family blessing, I prayed silently before eating, *Lord thank you for placing me in a land of opportunity among friends. Thank you for this day, the day you have made, and for the abundance of blessings you have provided in my life.*

Chapter 15

I LIVED WITH the Williams family during my schooling. At STCC I declared a minor in telecommunications to complement my Associate of Arts in General Studies program. The two years it took me to graduate seemed to fly by. The graduation ceremony was held at the Springfield Civic Center, and the keynote speaker was Secretary of State John Kerry, who at the time was US Attorney in Boston. Best of all, Tom travelled all the way from Africa just to attend my graduation. I had finally achieved my dream, and Tom was here to witness it. I knew in my heart and soul that it was God working through Tom. I watched as Tom took his seat near the front row. He sat up very straight with his ankle crossed over his knee. I watched him read the event program, and I saw a broad smile suddenly appear on his face as his body swayed with laughter. I wondered what made him smile so brightly. I made a mental note of exactly where he sat in the crowd. When my name was called, I rose up and I looked towards the direction he was seated. Our eyes met, and I maintained eye contact with him all the way up to the podium to receive my diploma.

After the ceremony, I walked over to where Tom was sitting and I handed him my diploma. Watching him study the cover reminded me of when I was issued my American student visa. It was a magical thing. Tears welled in my eyes and he said, "Francis you made it. I am proud of you." My heart sang at his words. I began to imagine ways that I could pay Tom back. I knew I could never make his dreams come true like he had done for me, but I thought perhaps I could both make him proud and pay him some of his money back. More than anything I was determined to show Tom that his kindness and attention had not been wasted on me. I had begun making plans to continue my education at the State University of New York. I knew Tom would respect my taking the initiative to pursue my goals. God answered my prayers and made my way clear.

Later that day I rode with Tom to the airport in Windsor Locks, Connecticut where he would begin his travels back to Africa. On the ride Tom told me to refrain from thanking him again for sponsoring me all these years. He had a suggestion for me. "Francis, this is important," he said. "If you ever one day have the capacity, you should consider helping another human being. Maybe another Sierra Leonean—though not necessarily the exact same way that I have helped you. But if you can, you should think about it." Once again Tom's words were etched on my heart.

I paid special attention to his every word. My thoughts were beginning to fill with scenarios in which I could help another human being. There was silence as Tom waited for my response. Before I could answer he continued, "Francis, I know America is not easy. You have yet to establish yourself. I don't want you to feel pressured. This is only a suggestion, an idea. If ever you have the capacity, you should do the same thing for another person. If you don't have the capacity, but you sincerely have the desire to do so, I believe that this will be sufficient for God."

I took a deep breath and told him that I would very much like to help another person someday. I shared my concern over my ability to help anyone outside of my extensive family that would someday be dependent on me.

He said, "I understand, because I have lived in Africa for a long time. But do what you can. Whatever it is will be fine. Serve God in all you do."

I never forgot his words. I still contemplate what it means to be a servant of God. Several times throughout my life I have been a recipient of His Grace through the kind deeds of others, and most frequently it would seem as if God worked to please me. As an adult I've come to recognize the importance of working to please God in both thought and deed. I think this is what Tom was trying to explain to me, so I try to keep God in my thoughts at all times.

With Tom's continued support I relocated to Brockport, New York where I attended SUNY, the State University of New York at Brockport.

After graduating with a bachelor's degree in communication arts, I returned to Springfield, Massachusetts, and enrolled in graduate studies at American International College, where I received a Master's of Arts in Public Administration with a minor in legal studies.

While I was enrolled in graduate studies at AIC, I worked as a personal care attendant in Amherst. This wasn't a job on my ultimate career path, but it was good experience and it provided me another opportunity to explore exciting and legendary sites, this time in the western portion of the United States. My employer Dan and I flew to Phoenix, Arizona to pick up a customized vehicle from a manufacturer designed to accommodate a client with disabilities. After we picked it up, we decided to explore the state of Arizona before heading back to Massachusetts. We decided to head south to the legendary, iconoclastic cowboy town of Tombstone. Dan and I spent the night on a camping site in the town of Benson. On the drive towards Tombstone, Dan pointed out a huge copper mine. I noticed the earth had been excavated in a round pattern with an opening about a mile wide and a mile around and at least as deep. I watched trucks pass along the sides of the wide open pit by driving along contours in the earth; the trucks drove around and around until they disappeared into the shadows. This mining operation was very different from what I'd witnessed in Sierra Leone. In Africa, digging for diamonds was largely done by heavy duty machines. The diamond filled dirt would be boxed and loaded to be taken to a separate location for sorting. I wondered what the actual miners in this copper mine looked like. How deep did that hole really go?

Upon arriving in Tombstone, Dan and I strolled through the open space and admired the buildings on Main Street. The town of Tombstone itself was no more than a handful of buildings and souvenir shops. We saw the site of the legendary gun fight, the O.K. Corral. We saw men dressed in complete cowboy attire: hats, boots, leather jackets and belts. The men were both walking and riding horses down Main Street. One solid black horse was draped with a large black leather saddle. It looked like a slice of midnight walking. Dan said the beautiful creature reminded him of the horse on the *Lone Ranger* television series. I told him I had no idea what he was talking about, to which he replied, "Let's go pet them."

I took a step away from him and folded my arms. I asked, "Are you well? Have you lost your mind? Animals are not for fun." Dan laughed uncontrollably. He kept saying he couldn't believe I was serious. Dan and I also visited the grave sites of famous cowboys who were shot and killed in gunfights.

The next day we drove north through Phoenix and headed for Las Vegas, Nevada. I was amazed by the landscape of southern Arizona. The landscape was splashed with vibrant features in the form of a variety of plants species. The terrain reminded me of the Sahara Desert, but here in Arizona the vegetation were mostly of a short variety. We stopped in the town of Flagstaff for refreshments and continued towards the Mojave Desert. As I drove north I began to see the vegetation slowly changing to shorter trees, and the green in the landscape diminished. Sand became ubiquitous, and distinguished from the road only by the painted lines. I was astonished. I never knew America had a desert. The road sign, "Now Approaching the Mojave Desert," was my first clue.

Dan and I camped out in the Mojave Desert that night. As I lay in the sand, I thought about my perilous trek across the world's deadliest desert that almost took my life. Here I was again sleeping out in the open desert. Whereas the Mojave had a few blades of grass and short trees, the Sahara had virtually no vegetation whatsoever, only sand and dry wind. We passed the night peacefully. Dan was concerned about wolves he claimed to hear howling in the distance. I soothed myself with the idea that it was the wind howling and I prayed, *God, please don't let me die in my sleep tonight. Thank you for this adventure and your grace that keeps both me and my companion safe. In the event you do not see fit to save me from the wolves that might come to eat me in the night, I'd like to say thank you for my life. In Jesus' name I pray.*

We survived the night and headed out to see the Hoover Dam. I continued to be baffled by the size of things in America. I gazed at the Hoover Dam, far down below which was a spectacular engineering facility, and I learned that the Hoover Dam provided electricity to several western states. I could see the Colorado River from afar, and I saw people kayaking.

We arrived in Las Vegas at night and I was shocked by the brightness of the city. It was the brightest lighting I had ever seen. We parked and walked along the Strip. As we ducked in and out of the lobbies of various hotels and casinos we witnessed thousands of people gathered in front of various gambling activity tables and machines. On the streets, which at 10pm were as bright as if the sun were out, a man walking by handed me pornographic leaflets. Colorfully dressed people got in and out of different limousines. I was invited to a musical show and solicited by a prostitute. Dan and I decided it was time to call it a night.

The next day we drove into the state of Utah. The people in Salt Lake City reminded me of the people in my village: they were peaceful and family-oriented. In a restaurant in Salt Lake City, I encountered several Mormon women with multiple young children. Both the women and the little girls were dressed in long dresses with head ties. I was in disbelief when Dan explained to me about the Mormon faith's open practice of polygamy. I had always thought that polygamous relationships were practiced only in African societies and among people of the Islamic faith. I didn't know how to process the incongruence between the American society I expected and the reality I was witnessing. I remembered the Bible warns, "Judge not lest ye be judged," and resolved to watch the children play.

My adventures through Utah took me to the Bryce Canyon and Zion National Parks. At both parks I was amazed at the spectacular natural phenomena. I observed different kinds of American wildlife. In Sierra Leone, everyone knows that wild animals are dangerous and no one purposefully goes into the bushes to admire their aesthetics. Standing at Zion National Park, I thought back to Gaby's wish to go on an African safari. I still cannot understand why people risk their lives to get close to wild animals. At any rate, my day at the parks was well spent: quality time with God's beautiful creations.

Our next stop was Wyoming, where we spent the night in Jackson Hole. The pristine natural environment immediately made me flash back to my visit to Mount Etna, in Sicily. I found myself standing at Old Faithful, thinking about the boiling hot lava under the earth's crust, remembering the volcanic eruptions on Mount Etna. There were several pools of bubbling hot springs boiling up to the surface. It looked to me like there was fire underneath the water which caused the water to boil with plumes of white steam. I overheard a geologist explaining that in a few hours there would be an eruption, so everyone stood waiting to see it. I did not stay to witness the action; I feared that the portion of the earth I was standing on might just collapse from underneath me. I could see myself submerged into a deep, boiling hot spring, thereby ending my life in the American national parks. I'd had similar thoughts when I visited Mount Etna. I asked God why he brought me to this place. What was God thinking when he came up with hot springs?

At this point in my life I was beginning to spread my wings in new and exciting ways. I routinely conducted inventories of God's blessings in my life. I added the sights of America to my long list. Tom had supported me in every way through my graduate studies. After I completed my master's degree we agreed that I no longer required his financial support, but we both also agreed that we would be friends for life.

Chapter 16

MY MEMORIES OF the years following my graduation from AIC
are marked by travel and loss. All my adventures were beginning to remind
me of home. I once again crossed the Atlantic to visit Africa.

After 15 years away from my mother, sisters and extended family in
Punduru, I missed my home and I longed to return to see my country. I had
kept in contact with my family through informal contacts with the few
Sierra Leoneans I knew who left the US and went home. During this period
my country lacked mobile telephone services, and my village did not have a
post office. Besides, my family did not know how to read or write. They
had never been out of my home region, and they spoke no language other
than Mende. Even if I could have gotten a letter to them, they would have
needed someone to read it to them. Though I knew my family knew I was
alive, and I also knew they were still alive, I had not talked to them personally for more than 10 years. I became especially eager to see my mother after all these years.

So in 1990, I returned to Sierra Leone on a visit for the first time since
I'd left in 1979. I was eager to go back and see the spot where Tom and I
met at the entrance to the predominantly white Yengema Club. On the
nine-hour flight from Boston through Amsterdam, I imagined what my
village would look like. I looked forward to seeing the huge orange tree at
the village's center. I wondered if it was time for initiations, or if there was
some other reason to celebrate. I reflected over my life: how God had
blessed me with Tom, who rescued me and changed my life; I thought of

my impoverished background and hardships, my worldly adventures and experiences, and my new home in America. I was fully prepared to narrate my adventures, as I knew my family would be full of questions. Yes, this time I could tell them I found a diamond ... of sorts.

As I sat on the KLM flight to Sierra Leone I experienced a mixture of emotions ranging from the gratitude that God had smiled on me, to fear and embarrassment at what lay ahead of me. I was acutely aware of my family's extreme poverty, and although I was coming from America, I was fresh out of school and did not have any extra money to give to my family. I assumed that they would expect me to come bearing gifts, and to have plenty of cash in my pocket. I knew that my family wouldn't turn me away just because I was still poor, but I felt a strange pain at the idea of disappointing them in any way.

As the pilot announced our landing at Freetown Lungi International Airport, a joyful feeling suddenly flowed over me as I gazed through the window and saw the palm trees, huts, houses with rusted corrugated zinc tops, and bushes and trees below. I managed to look to the far left across the aisle of the jetliner and gaze at Freetown and the Atlantic Ocean below as the airplane touched down.

The trip from Freetown to Punduru took a whole day. The way to my village largely lacks passable roads and passes through the town of Jaiama Sewafe, a region in the Kono District commonly referred to as the diamond zone of Sierra Leone. My family was shocked and surprised, but nonetheless excited to see me. Everyone cried and shouted. The children came in from the field when my sister yelled, "Your uncle is here!" My mother could not stop touching my face. She hugged me, stepped back to look at me, and then hugged me again. Bettie, especially, could not stop crying.

The townspeople came to my house as news spread that I was home from America. My mother asked me endless questions and I did my very best to explain and answer most of them. My family was curious about Tom. I told them stories about all that had happened to me since I left.

My people had obviously heard about America and England and they were now eager to hear everything about America from me. One of my nieces said, "Is it true that America is the home of the white man, where people live good lives, where almost everything is in abundance, plentiful money and where one can easily find work for good wages, a place you can excel and get opportunity?" I laughed, trying to buy myself time to answer.

I began explaining the differences and the similarities between America and Sierra Leone. "America is just like any other place on earth. But the main difference," I explained, "is that America is a highly developed, industrialized society." Everyone stared back at me with blank looks on their faces. I couldn't think of a way to help them understand, let alone relate to, the idea of what a developed, industrialized society looks like. I tried to proceed in the simplest comparative terms available by relating my points to my people's environment and lifestyle.

My family responded "What?" in unison when I told them about the weather conditions in America, how it gets very cold with snow in the winter, and scalding hot in the summer. I explained that in America, the government builds and maintains roads, provides free primary and secondary education to all its children, and the many other things the government does for its people in exchange for taxes. Their jaws dropped. I explained, "Nothing in America is really free. America is expensive, and you must pay for almost everything."

In the two and half weeks that I was home I observed that the landscape and vegetation had been significantly altered. The once thick forests with gigantic trees surrounding the narrow dirt road between Jaiama Sewafe and my village had provided a cool canopy of foliage, but they had now withered and disappeared. The forest bushes surrounding my village were slowly disappearing. The gigantic trees where the monkeys used to spring from one branch to another had all withered, and only a few trees remained standing. The streams that once flowed in the forest around Punduru were drying up, and where there used to be different kinds of birds singing, I hardly saw any birds at all.

The land that was once my mother's small garden and plantation, where she cultivated bananas, coffee and cacao, now lay bare. When I asked my mother why, she told me that over the years they had experienced unusually hot and prolonged dry seasons with little or no rain. The crops died, and she was unable to resuscitate the land.

The only environmental activity that remained unchanged over the years was the sustained low-level gold and diamond mining along the Sewa

River. Scores of people, men and women presumably from other parts of Sierra Leone, had relocated and were encamped along the Sewa River, to work in gold and diamond mining. Some of my extended family members were also engaged in the low-level mining, but my people did not have the financial resources and investment required to undertake profitable mining. The fact that so many people were still digging for gold and diamonds along the Sewa River proves true the saying, "Diamonds are forever."

I left Punduru and went to Gaia Camp in Yengema, where I met up with Alfred. Word had already spread that I had arrived from America, so he was expecting me. I was looking forward to seeing him. I found him and his family in the same one-bedroom NDMC squatter mining camp house I'd left them in. When I first laid eyes on him I wanted to cry and ask him why he had treated me so badly. I had to push away the anger and resentment I still felt.

I stayed with Alfred for three days. I did my best to suppress and ignore unpleasant memories that came flooding into my mind, but unfortunately, every negative experience came back and resonated with me emotionally—particularly when I found myself sitting down in the chair on the same veranda floor I was once laid on and beaten. I recalled the conversations I had with Tom years ago in Greece regarding Alfred. Tom had advised me then to learn to forgive, and I never forgot that advice. Standing in front of Alfred I continued to be ambivalent about forgiving a man who beat me so often for no apparent reason.

My first evening there I sat listening to Alfred talk about his work in the mines as I tried to plan my words wisely. I did not want to make Alfred feel bad, or to embarrass him. I didn't come for revenge. I felt like if I could manage to say the words the stone tied to my heart might be released. I knew in my spirit that it was the right time to let him know that I had forgiven him. I knew he was sincerely and genuinely excited to see me again, and he treated me with respect and as his dignified guest of honor. My cousin gave up his bedroom for me, insisting that I must sleep in his bed as his guest of honor. He spent the three nights with his wife and children boarding with a neighbor.

I sensed my cousin genuinely made his best efforts within his meager means to accommodate me and to make me feel at home. Whether or not he ever thought of apologizing to me I cannot say, but I never expected it. In retrospect, during the time I lived with him I clearly remember a man who was under significant duress due to the tremendous responsibilities he'd assumed. He had a whole household that was wholly and absolutely dependent upon him for their entire sustenance and survival. His meager salary was never enough to even feed his family, and he took on the burden of an extra child, me.

On the second day I went for a walk with Alfred towards the NDMC headquarters. He explained NDMC had changed, that all the Europeans had gone back to England and that NDMC was now owned and operated exclusively by the government of Sierra Leone. He repeatedly asked about Tom. As we walked past the Separator House, I seized the moment. I stepped into Alfred's way so that I was facing him and I grabbed both of his hands. Surely the look on my face let him know that I had something important thing to say. I locked my eyes onto his and said, "I am sorry that you treated me badly before." I don't know where the words came from. I simply said what was on my heart. We continued to hold hands, and he nodded his head. Without warning my tears dried up and I became uncomfortable. I released his hands and quickly changed the subject. I began telling him how very cold it is in some parts of America, explaining the weather conditions in the winters, the people, foods, houses, etc.

On the third day of my visit with Alfred in Gaia Camp, I walked from the camp past the Separator House into the NDMC administrative headquarters towards the Yengema Club. I was shocked to see the Separator House was now an abandoned warehouse. It was no longer a fortified facility with barbed wire. The building that once housed millions, perhaps billions, of dollars of diamonds was now deserted and abandoned, with elephant grass all around it. I was still eager and curious to go back to the site where Tom had met me sitting down at the entrance of the Yengema Club, selling oranges. As I walked past the Electric Power Generator House, which was still in operation, I noted fewer than 20 African staffers and personnel in the administrative offices. Those offices that were once filled with high level administrative officers, most of whom were Europeans, had notably changed as I saw not a single white man. I noticed other departments, like motor transport, along with townships and stores, were all shut down with the doors and windows boarded. As I continued walking in the direction of the racquet court adjacent to the supermarket, the Yengema Club came into view. It was now an abandoned warehouse surrounded by tall elephant grass. The area that was once a parking lot around the club was now covered with weeds and tall grasses. I gazed at what was once the golf course where professional tournaments were once frequently played. The landscape was now only tall bushes, and the grounds were covered with different kinds of vegetation.

Alfred was correct about the drastically deteriorated state of NDMC mining operations in my country. I went on to visit the town of Koidu, the district headquarters and where I had bought my first pair of shoes. I remember Koidu being filled with foreigners from as far away as from Mali, Senegal, Gambia, Liberia, Syria, Lebanon, and Guinea. I assumed it was the diamonds that drew so many people into the crowded town. Now there was a greatly reduced Lebanese presence and there appeared to be few business transactions taking place.

I returned back to my village and said goodbye to my family before returning to the United States. I had to accept a hard truth when preparing to end my visit. This would be the last time I would see my mother, as she was now late in years. She spoke to me as sweetly as she did when I was a boy, telling me, "Love me wherever you are and I will know. Speak to God and he will speak to my heart." It was a tearful parting, even harder this time. I felt like this time was different, like I might never step foot on this land again. The idea made me miserable. In spite of the deterioration and major changes, Punduru remained, in my mind, picturesque.

Little did I know that just one year later, Sierra Leone would plunge into the most brutal and savage rebel war that the world had ever seen. The war would last for 10 years, during which the most heinous crimes would be committed, and it would take a multi-international force to quell the most senseless rebel war in history. As I followed the news coverage about the violence in Sierra Leone, I cried imagining my mother, sisters and their children caught in the crossfire. I prayed to God asking that he watch over my loved ones. *God, why is there war? Please rain peace onto the situation in Sierra Leone. Protect my loved ones. Keep them safe from harm. Thank you for blessing me and keeping me.*

God answered my prayer. None of my family was lost to direct rebel violence. Unfortunately my mother was not able to survive life in the forest high above the mountains. I got word from cousins living in Michigan that my mother died in her sleep. I imagined my mother exhausted from trying to farm or search out roots for her remedies in the rocky forest. I imagined a lot of climbing and walking that I'm sure my mother did not back down from, not even in her advanced years. It was odd that nothing about my everyday life changed after the news, but inside everything was different. I carried a hope of being reunited with my mother in my heart that had to die with her. I would never see my mother again. To my mind, my mother's physical location in Sierra Leone marked that I still had a home to return to. Without her, home faded into memories of a place we used to live, one to which I could never find my way back. The hole left in my heart after losing my mother could never be filled.

Upon returning to the States, I received a letter from Tom telling me that he had been offered a job at the U.S. State Department in the Drug Enforcement Agency (DEA), stationed in Lima, Peru. The goal was to stop drug production and the flow of drugs to the United States. But the big news was that he'd met a young Peruvian Indian girl and that they'd had a baby boy. The next letter I received from Tom relayed more major life events. He said that they'd had another child, a girl, and that he had returned to flying for Viking Helicopters in West Africa on a contract from the World Health Organization, eradicating river blindness in West Africa. I knew his job as a helicopter pilot for the DEA in Peru had been risky and very dangerous. I was very happy for him and his family, and happy that he'd left South America and the DEA.

Sadly for me, the bus ride from Springfield to Bradley International Airport on the day of my graduation turned out to be the last time I would ever see Tom. My world came crumbling down when Tom's ex-girlfriend Shauana, who was now living in California, wrote me a letter and told me that Tom had suffered a massive heart attack and passed away in the West African nation of Togo, leaving behind a wife and two young children. I'd gotten the news too late to attend his funeral services in Milaca, Minnesota.

My friend and benefactor Thomas Frederick Johnson died in December of 1993 at the young age of 44. His casket was flown from Lome, Togo, to Minneapolis, Minnesota and interred at the Forest Hills cemetery in his hometown of Milaca, Minnesota.

For a long time I sorted my thoughts according to whether they related to Tom or not. I lost my appetite and I had trouble sleeping. I could not deny I was depressed. I tried to pray but the words didn't come. I continued my job working for the City of Springfield Public Schools, but I felt terribly guilty because I was not at Tom's funeral to thank him for and speak about his generosity, to thank him for changing my life, for his altruism, and for giving me such a golden opportunity. The regret haunted me for very long time.

In 1995, a friend I'd met in Springfield told me about a job opportunity in Puerto Rico. Though I was quite hesitant to go at first, with help from a friend whose relatives resided in Aguadilla, Puerto Rico, I made the trip. My friend's family was very helpful to me. They assisted me in renting a house for only $200 per month. Once I started living there, I discovered that Puerto Rico is a beautiful island with its own unique culture.

Before long I became an English language teacher in the Escuela Jose de Diego, in Aguadilla, even though I did not speak a single word of Spanish. Conversational Italian, casual Greek, I'm your man, but Spanish was a new venture. Quite frankly, I was amazed that I was hired to be an English language teacher to a group of Spanish speaking students.

I found Puerto Rico to be quite an interesting island. This time I was not the only black person in the area. In fact, I noted that there were many people who were Puerto Rican but looked African. I recalled the Trans-Atlantic slave trade and the repatriation of slaves back to Africa. I knew there were black people in Jamaica, Trinidad, Cuba and Haiti, but I'd never thought of blacks in Puerto Rico.

The beaches of Puerto Rico reminded me of the beaches in Greece and in Gioia Tauro, in Italy. The restaurant on the beachfront in Aguadilla called to mind the tavern on the beachfront in Tolon, where Tom and I had a lengthy conversation regarding my travel plans to the United States.

My stay in Puerto Rico was cut short after the deadly Hurricane Georges powerfully swept through the island, wreaking havoc. I had heard of hurricanes but I had never experienced the fury of one. I imagined the storm brewing over the Sahara, and the prevailing winds giving rise to Georges. I was amazed at nature's interconnectedness.

Although I'd made a lot of friends in Puerto Rico, including the mayor of Aguadilla, who was such a friendly man, it was time to return to the United States. I learned of a job as a Care Coordinator for Wraparound Milwaukee Services in Wisconsin. I liked the idea of a job where I could help people. I applied and was hired, and landed in Milwaukee in 1998.

Three years later I took a job as Probation and Parole Agent with the State of Wisconsin, Department of Corrections in the Milwaukee office. To assuage my guilty conscience for not being present at Tom's funeral years past, as soon as I joined the Corrections team I immediately transferred to the office in Hayward, since it was closer to Tom's mother, Virginia.

I made it my duty to visit her frequently. She was then in her early eighties. Every other weekend, I drove to Milaca on Saturday and stayed in Tom's bedroom. She was a devout Baptist, so we attended church service together on Sunday morning. We grew very close. I fondly remembered her sending me packages of clothes and other things back in Sierra Leone, and the many letters she had written me over the years. Having Virginia Johnson in my life was the next best thing to being able to see my own mother.

Chapter 17

TOM'S ABSENCE IN my life came with a loss of the feeling of protection that comes with knowing someone cares about you. I'd gotten married to my first American girlfriend, and the relationship disintegrated within three years' time. When I first moved to Hayward, I often felt lonely even when surrounded by other people. Visiting Virginia went a long way towards healing my mourning heart. Another factor in my healing was the Native American community on the Lac Courte Oreilles reservation (LCO). With the Native Americans I found a new zest for life and a camaraderie that I had not enjoyed since my years in Greece. Along with that friendship came a deepening of my understanding of the complexity of American culture, society, and history. Coming from Sierra Leone, I had a view of America as a place of unlimited possibility. I remember Tom telling me, "In America if you work hard, if you go to school and get an education, you can have a good chance of making it." I'd felt blessed by God when I landed a state job. I had to learn the hard way that life in America is complex. Life in Hayward would mark the conversion of my long-held American dream into a nightmare.

Hayward is located in one of the most virgin regions of northern Wisconsin. The pristine forests and lakes provide a perfect getaway from the twin cities of Minneapolis and St. Paul and attract the rich of northern Illinois. During the treacherous and unforgiving winters in Hayward, swarms of hunters come in search of deer. Summers in Hayward routinely see a caravan of very expensive new cars roll into town, as the rich seek to escape the pace of urban life.

Hayward is also the home of the Ojibwa Native American tribe, situated on the LCO, which is the largest reservation among the band of Chippewa Indians of Northern Wisconsin, as well as in the Great Lakes region of Canada and the United States. The LCO is on beautiful, green forested land. It features pristine hills and flat lands with thick forests and deer and bear running wild. One of the most amazing aspects of the reservation is its political system. Like other reservations, I soon came to know that LCO is a sovereign nation and not considered a territory of the United States. The LCO tribal government consists of nine council members, all elected by registered Native American voters. I came to personally know six of the nine tribal council members. Rusty Barber, a council member who was also a relative of my landlady Rose, had served in the United States military in Germany, and he and I became good friends.

There was something about contact with the Ojibwa people that made me feel adventurous. I had spent much of my adult life exploring and experiencing places, cultures and peoples. My previous encounters with new cultures were always guided by friends I made along the way. I was concerned that I didn't know anyone, but I was so eager to experience new languages and foods that I resolved to work around my shyness and make new friends.

Once again I got lucky. I met a woman named Rosanne Barber who was full Ojibwa. Rose and her sister Val owned acres of land on the reservation. The land had been passed to them by their father, who was once a tribal judge. The Barbers had a long standing reputation on the LCO; in fact, there is a whole section of the reservation that is called Barber Town. Rose rented me a house located directly behind her own home in the heart of the forested section of the reservation for only $300 per month.

Rose and her extended family were excited to have me living amongst them. They routinely entertained and fed me. I was simultaneously a guest of honor and an accepted member of the family. Native American culture had a spiritual richness to it that was missing from so many other cultures I'd encountered. I felt a true kinship not just with Rose's family, but with all of the Ojibwa of Hayward.

Members of the tribe introduced me to new leisure activities, including wild rice harvesting and sword fishing. One of my most novel experiences was ice fishing. My friends and I set out early on a Saturday morning in our galoshes with a drill machine, an axe and fishing rods. I was nervous as we stepped from the shore onto the frozen ice. I slipped and fell and was ready to call it a day. My friends helped me up after they had laughed heartily. We ventured about 15 feet away from the shore and chose a spot in the ice. One of the men knelt down and struck the ice and then began drilling with a machine to reach the water below. The circle grew to about 12" in diameter. The men began to cheer, and I wondered what so exciting. Before I knew it I was being ushered to the hole, which I approached cautiously. I envisioned the ice cracking and the lake swallowing me into its icy depths. I'd drown, trapped beneath the ice. No, thank you. Before I could turn and head back for land, another man shoved a fishing pole in my hand. "Fish," they all began to chant. I was caught by their excitement and cast my line down the hole. Before long I felt a sudden tension as if someone were trying to snatch the fishing rod from my hands. The others helped me reel in the fish. It was unlike any experience I'd had. That night we had a bonfire and cooked the fish over the open flames.

I became a fixture in the Ojibwa community. I knew and was well known at the administrative tribal offices, at the schools, the health department, the credit unions and, above all, the LCO casino. I became well-known both on the reservation and in the town of Hayward. The Ojibwa became quite interested in and curious about me, because I was black and from Africa. I was often asked if I was related to Nelson Mandela. "He's from a country south of mine," I would say. In conversations they would admire me because I'd come to America and gone to school and then got a government job. I was often told how delighted they were to have a minority working there, since almost all the other law enforcement officers were white. My high visibility could be attributed to that fact that I was the only professional black person in a town where there were hardly any black people visible at all. I especially stood out because I was a probation and parole agent.

At first I liked and enjoyed working in the Hayward Probation office. I was constantly asked by white people why I had chosen to come to

Hayward. Natives in the community couldn't understand why anyone would volunteer to live in Hayward. My job as a probation officer regularly required me to drive through the forests to my clients' homes; this was one of the several aspects of my employment in Hayward that I cherished most, especially in the summer months. In the summer, the trees grew thick with leaves. Some of the most peaceful times of my life were spent driving through the silent forests under the thick canopy of trees, with streams and creeks nearby, with deer and bears everywhere, and they stand out among my worldwide adventures. The pristine forest in Hayward reminded me of the forest that surrounded my village in Punduru, but I was completely shocked when told by my native friends that the snakes in the forest in Hayward were not poisonous and do not bite. Although I wondered why the snakes in my village had been deadly and these were not, I was relieved that I did not have to be on constant lookout for snakes in the forest in Hayward.

My experiences with the Italians in Gioia Tauro had prepared me to be the only black person in town. What it had not prepared me for was being immersed in a region where two communities lived side by side in a symbiotic relationship. I came to understand that the relationship between whites and Native Americans was always a delicate one that could quickly turn into acrimony and/or confrontation within the blink of an eye. I witnessed the delicate relationship firsthand, grudges and grievances each community held against the other.

My conversations with Native friends often began with some perceived wrong committed by a white person around town, and then it quickly escalated to a discussion of the injustices they had endured as a people, including losing their lands to the white people. I sat in on a conversation with Rose's family about white people. The men and women were in an uproar over the historical and present violations committed against them. They cried out, "I don't like them!" "They took my land!" "They killed my people!" and "They told us we cannot harvest our own timber!" I was looking for a point of entry into the conversation, so I asked, "Who told you not to harvest your timber?"

A nephew leaned forward in his seat at the kitchen table, and with a plain face answered, "The American government." Then he began to chronicle various treaties and how the United States had violated the treaties with the Indian Nations. He continued, "They did the same thing to you in Africa!" His words resonated with me. Even as a youth I had always felt that there was something inherently wrong about how the Europeans reserved the best parts of Sierra Leone's diamond harvest for themselves. I had a new appreciation for the tension that existed between white people and Native Americans.

I caught a glimpse of the flip-side of the coin with my white neighbors. I enjoyed good relationships with several prominent individuals in Hayward's white community. They, too, were curious about my skin, my heritage, my voyage to America, and my education, and I didn't mind sharing some of the details of my life. I soon realized that the white citizens of Hayward also held grievances and peculiar views about the Natives, which often played out in grudge matches.

During my numerous interactions with individuals in the white community, conversations often led to comments and/or complaints, like, "They don't pay any taxes!" "They get everything for free!" and "We pay the taxes and they get the free money!" were common. The clerk at the gas station in Hayward warned me in no uncertain terms not to associate with the Natives for several reasons. I wondered what the man would think if he knew that I lived with the Natives on their reservation, and that I spent leisure time and dined with them regularly.

In Hayward I was reluctant to get too engaged in the white bashing or Indian bashing. I learned to maintain a delicate balance with my friends and neighbors. However, my high visibility and close proximity to the Ojibwa community presented a conflict of interest at my employment for the State of Wisconsin. Approximately 80% of the offenders on active supervision on my caseload were my Ojibwa neighbors. There was absolutely no conceivable way I could have avoided interacting with my Native American clients on a regular basis while residing on their reservation. My auto mechanic on the reservation was a client. I ran into clients in the grocery stores and at the trading post.

One day I was sitting in the Snowshoe Saloon, a place nestled in some trees not far from my house, along County Highway B. The family-owned bar was a small, white bungalow converted into a saloon. Like in most of the reservation facilities and businesses, there were seldom any white people in this bar. Just on the other side of the wooden entry door there was an open area with tables, chairs, and a jukebox. The walls were covered with original Native American artwork. In the back, a bedroom had been converted into a pool room, with dart boards hanging on the walls. Rusty Barber and I were laughing over beers while he was telling me his experiences in the US Army in Germany when a six-foot tall young man of about 25 years of age entered the bar and headed for our table. He wore an oversized, checkered flannel jacket and yellow work boots. I studied the young man for several seconds before recognizing him as one of my clients. Much to my surprise, when Rusty saw the young man he rose from the table and embraced him. They greeted one another before turning to me. Rusty said, "Francis, this is my little cousin Mike."

I said, "I know Mike," with a smile and extended my hand for him to shake. The smile fell off Mike's face as he said, "You're that P.O. I just got assigned. Yeah. How're you doing?"

I was at a loss for words. Why was this offender in a bar in the first place, when his rules of supervision clearly prohibited him from entering bars and from consuming alcohol? When Rusty invited Mike to join us my heart sank into my stomach. I could feel my eyes open as wide as possible and my jaw drop. I tried to subtly signal Rusty to withdraw the invitation. Fortunately Mike declined, saying he was there to meet a friend. Mike said his goodbyes and disappeared into the pool room.

"What's wrong with you," Rusty asked once we were alone. I cracked the shell on a peanut and studied the red skin inside. I tried to slow the thoughts that were racing in my mind. I was going over the departmental zero tolerance policy for fraternization with offenders in my head. I sat there thinking about how great it was to be experiencing Ojibwa culture and traditions, but that my job basically precluded me from interacting with my neighbors even when not official duty. Something had to be done if I wanted to keep my job.

I finally answered Rusty, telling him, "That was a close call for me." Rusty raised his eyebrows and held up one finger signaling me to wait before speaking more. He called out to the bartender for another round then turned back to me and said, "How so?"

I explained to Rusty that if his cousin had sat down with us, I would have been breaking the departmental fraternization policy. I went on, "And if he had taken a drink in front of me I would have had to hold him accountable for rules violations, which would include holding him in custody while I investigated the violations. In fact, I think I'm going to call it a night. If he comes out of that pool room with a beer in his hand, I'll have to … Well you know. So good night." I shifted in my chair to reach in my back pocket for my wallet to pay my tab, and Rusty leaned forward and slowly lowered his right palm onto the table. He said, "Thank you, Francis. If you were a white cop, Mike would be in handcuffs and on his way to jail just for walking into the door. I understand that you just want to live in peace and do your job. I don't know how you can manage it, man."

"Honestly, until this incident tonight I felt like I was handling it on my own. But now I think I will look into an exemption," I said, putting my jacket on.

Rusty walked me to my car and bid me good night.

The next day I asked my immediate supervisor for a meeting and explained the circumstances of my close relationship with the Native Americans due to my living situation. I was granted the exemption, but as a condition I was precluded from discussing any work-related issues and concerns with any of my clients outside of work.

The exemption gave me some peace of mind when going about my daily affairs. I couldn't shake what Rusty had said about if I were a white cop. I went over the scenario again and again. I was acutely aware of the fact that most of the clients on my caseload had committed their crimes while under the influence of liquor. It was possible that Mike had no intention of consuming alcohol, but the idea that a parole officer would violate someone just for being in the proximity of cause for violation was beyond what I could embrace as "right." The only thing I would have done differently that night before leaving would be to give Mike a direct order to leave the bar immediately, refrain from consuming alcohol, and to report to my office at 8am the next day.

After two years in Hayward, I had learned how to navigate both the injustices and the joys of living and working with the Native and white communities of Hayward. During the Thanksgiving holiday that year I had an epiphany. What if, like the time of the first Thanksgiving, natives and white people came together? I told Rose my idea and she told me she didn't see it happening within our lifetime. I was absolutely obsessed with the idea. I sat down and started writing about all the injustices in human history. I came to the conclusion that no race or government is perfect. No matter the prior wrongdoings, I felt an overwhelming sense of gratitude for my place in life and in the US. To express my appreciation for the generosity accorded to me by the Native American community in Hayward, I wrote a letter to the editor of the Sawyer County Record newspaper in Hayward. My letter was published on December 1, 2004:

Dear Editor,

I am a recent immigrant to this nation, and I voted for the first time in the 2004 presidential elections. I write to express my gratitude and appreciation during this Thanksgiving season for the enormous opportunities this nation has to offer me and countless other immigrants, including those arrived in the New World even before the Separatists (pilgrims) landed on Plymouth, Massachusetts in 1620. The Separatists on the Plymouth plantation owed their survival exclusively to the goodwill and generosity of their neighbors, the Wampanoag native Indians of Cape Cod. The pilgrims so courageously demonstrated their values and Protestant work ethic at the end of that treacherous winter of 1620 by expressing gratitude, thereby establishing the tradition of the Thanksgiving ceremony in this country. As a newly acculturated immigrant, I am honored to have celebrated this year's Thanksgiving with my Lac Courte Oreilles Ojibwa neighbors, families and friends in Hayward. And whereas the Separatists were taught the essential skills of fishing, hunting and crop farming by their Massachusetts Wampanoag Indian neighbors, which ensured their survival the winter of 1620, my Wisconsin Ojibwa kinsmen and women have been very generous to me, this newly arrived immigrant. That is what I reckon Thanksgiving may be all about on both an individual and a collective basis.

I don't know if it was because of my Ojibwa friends, but my eyes had been opened. I had a new appreciation for the minority group grievances with the dominant white culture. I began to see abuses of power at every turn. I noticed disproportionate conviction rates for Native American clients when compared to other ethnicities. I noticed Native American clients were held in custody longer, and frequently their probation and parole cases were revoked for minor rules violations. I still recall specific cases where, in response to minor rules violations that clearly required only a verbal warning, I was required by my supervisor to hold Native American offenders in custody and eventually initiate proceedings for revocation of their probation and or parole statuses. The treatment of Native American offenders in the Hayward DOC office was so blatantly prejudicial that a public defender once lamented to me that the Hayward office led the number of received revocation cases.

I was conflicted. I did not know how to process the things I was seeing. Otherwise good men were committing human rights violations right before my eyes. I feared for my job if I objected to how others were doing their jobs, so I focused on being the best officer I could. I continued to be grateful for my life in America, even as I accepted the imperfections in American culture and history. My job required that I learn about the American constitution, its jurisprudence, and the structures of federal, state and local governments. As I read I fell in love with America's design, its functional institutions, structures and processes and the mechanisms designed for addressing civil, criminal, and human rights grievances. I understood that the lack of such a system of checks and balances was what kept Sierra Leone and villages like Punduru in third world status. Installing a Congress could probably help circumvent the chronic corruptions in the government of Sierra Leone. I developed the conviction that the United States was the leading country in the world, with a robust, functioning governmental system designed to provide opportunities for its citizens to be heard and maintain a functional judicial system for redressing human grievances, including upholding due process.

With a state job, I was convinced that I was now on the path to experiencing the American dream. As a law enforcement officer in the Hayward

DOC office, I was sworn to both employ confidentiality and to uphold the laws of the State of Wisconsin and the laws of the United States. I found myself in the awkward position of having knowledge of prejudicial treatment, but being unable to tell the victims. I tried to reconcile my personal convictions with my professional duties to little avail. While I was preoccupied with protecting the rights of others, a strange and unexpected twist was about to come my way, one that would change the direction of my life.

Chapter 18

I HAD HEARD about the racist treatment of black people in America, but I hadn't witnessed or experienced it myself. The days spanning the winter months of 2005 to the spring of 2014 were marked by heartache and humiliation for me as I was indoctrinated into the dark side of the American justice system.

My experiences have taught me that although perpetrators may be motivated by racial prejudice, their tactics are those of bullies. I'd had plenty of experience with bullies—my cousin Alfred and the boys at my secondary school in Yengema. In each situation I felt myself small, pitted against an opponent twice my size. The brute strength of the bully all too often ensured my compliance with the bully's demands. In the case of the Hayward prosecutor and my employer, I stood up for myself for a change.

During my first two years in Hayward I came to develop a sense of permanence for the first time since my childhood days in Punduru. I had friends and work and Virginia. I often prayed, *God, thank you for my life in a country many worlds away from my birthplace. Thank you for the opportunities you have afforded me. I hope to be worthy of your grace and favor. Amen.* At work I was respected. I worked in concert with three other probation and parole agents to supervise offenders on probation, parole and extended supervision. I never entertained the possibility that years of camaraderie, shared dedication to the job, and my deep personal satisfaction could come to an abrupt end.

One morning my supervisor handed me a sealed envelope, addressed to me. He threw the letter on my desk and walked out without explanation. My heart began to race. What could it be? Rather than speculate I soldiered past my racing heartbeat and opened the envelope. I began to read a list of alleged employment rules violations. I was in disbelief. The world began to close in around me. I couldn't make sense of what I was reading. My job had become an intricate part of who I was, and according to this notice, I had failed. My sense of self-worth collapsed.

A slew of the alleged work rules violations and investigations went on for months. In the meantime I was concerned about drawing more fury from my employer, so I withdrew from social activities and began spending evenings alone, on my computer. I still recall those emotionally raw days. I was mourning the death of Tom and my marriage. I was homesick and lonely. Spending time in chat rooms functioned as a form of temporary distraction. It was there that I met Jessica. She introduced herself as being from Liverpool, England. Everything about her sounded appealing to me. I was so excited to be having a real exchange with someone who knew nothing of my woes. Small talk grew into meaningful conversation, punctuated with cultural jokes and comparisons.

Jessica and I fell in love. After weeks of sharing photos, personal histories, phone conversations, and our views of the world, no doubt remained in my mind that I had found the woman for me, and that this was meant to be.

I was anxious to meet Jessica in person. I explained that I could not leave the country right then due to work matters. Jessica said she could come to the US right away. Well, almost right away. Jessica was the only daughter of the owner of a flourishing international textiles business. She told me that her family had several clothing outlets located in the US. Jessica's loyalty to her family was unbounded, and her parents insisted that my intentions be tested in some way. She proposed an idea: she would have one of her father's clothing outlets mail $4,000 in U.S. Postal Money orders to me, and I would then wire her the cash. I thought that her strategy of proving my intentions was odd. This seemed like a test to see if I would steal, not if I would treat their daughter well. I reasoned that it was a straightforward transaction, and I was in love.

My desire for Jessica grew every day. The relationship felt strong; our feelings for one another felt genuine. I hoped that completing the test would quash her family's doubts. I eagerly searched my mailbox every day until the envelope arrived. I signed into the chat room and informed Jessica that the money orders had arrived. I cashed the $4,000 in money orders at our local grocer, Market Place Foods in Hayward, and wired all the funds through Western Union to London. After emailing her the Western Union control number, I awaited her receipt of the cash and with it confirmation of my honorable intentions.

Up until then, my life held fading memories of relationships found and lost. The soft flowing voice of love had finally found me, and I was struck with deep emotions in a relationship promising newfound intimacy, faithfulness and devotion. We made plans to meet: she would fly to Minneapolis, and I would welcome her to my corner of the world. As June approached, the date of our meeting grew near. I received an email from Jessica. She assured me of her trust, but there still, somehow, remained a family reservation. She explained that she would send me a second set of money orders from one of her family's outlets, and I would then cash them and wire the funds to London again.

I stared at the screen for a long time. Although I was blind in love, I couldn't help but sense that something was wrong. I couldn't put my finger on it. How many times would I have to repeat this exercise before I gained their trust? Why couldn't they cash their own money orders? I tried to soothe myself with the idea that the point of the exercise was not the money. I had already proven that Jessica was worth far more than material wealth. On the telephone Jessica reassured me and insisted that once she received the cash, she could leave for the US in two days.

My heart strings were bound to this woman who loved me so deeply and whom I wanted passionately. Within days I received the next set of postal money orders totaling $5,000. An eerie feeling crept over me as I held the money orders. Again I asked myself how not stealing the money orders would show that I had good intentions towards their daughter. A host of possibilities flooded my mind. I decided to deposit the money orders into my checking account, and I had the teller make copies of the money orders. After four days, I withdrew the $5,000 and wired it to

London. Though I had a sense that something was amiss, I still held onto the hope that Jessica would be in my arms within a couple days.

Sometimes there is no clear reason for what we do, and this was one of those times. Jessica's adamant yet loving plea that I send her cash the second time had hurt me in some vague way. The doubt that had crept in at the last minute was almost suspicion; it felt staged. I phoned her to let her know the money had been wired, but that I was withholding the Western Union control number until I had submitted the copies of the money orders to the United States Postal Service for authentication. Jessica immediately began screaming and cursing at me. Hearing her talk to me with such animosity cut straight to my heart. This couldn't be her, insulting my integrity and accusing me of stealing her money. She vowed never to come to the US and hung up the phone.

Jessica's behavior put the last nail in our relationship's coffin. I was heartbroken again. Still, I had another urgent concern. If I was right, then there was something fraudulent about the money orders. Painful as it was, I reluctantly drove to the post office with the copies in order to verify what I did not want to face. Yes, the money orders were counterfeit. Betrayal and fear filled me like never before. I had been scammed into these illegal transactions by the excitement of a new romance. I instantly became concerned about my employer's response to my involvement in these transactions.

I drove to my bank realizing there was little chance of undoing this horrendous blunder. I asked for Susan, one of the managers. She appeared at the edge of the lobby and beckoned me into her office. I immediately sat down in one of the chairs and threw my head back with both my palms outstretched. I said. "Susan, I am in embarrassing trouble." Beads of sweat collected on my forehead, and I picked up a bank information pamphlet from the corner of her desk and began to fumble with it. She waited a few seconds then asked, "How may I help you, Mr. Mandewah?"

A few other bank employees began to gather in her office. Trembling and sweating profusely, I realized there was no way out but to recount every embarrassing detail to those who were now present in the office.

"The money orders that I deposited a few days ago into my bank account were fake," I said bluntly. I proceeded to narrate my whole unfortunate ordeal.

Her reaction was matter-of-fact. "First, we must wait for the money orders to process through our clearing house. Let's give this a couple of days."

After signing some paperwork, I immediately crossed the street to Market Place Foods. My intention was straightforward: I would explain the same unfortunate and embarrassing situation to the store's manager. I would retrieve the $5,000 that was held by Western Union but never delivered to Jessica from the second transaction. I would use the money to reimburse the store its $4,000 from the first transaction and return the balance to the bank.

I crossed the street and entered the Market Place Foods store and Detective Mark Kelsey of Hayward PD stepped in behind me. I knew Mark from work. He frequently picked up offenders at my office and took them to jail. Mark's demeanor was odd: he didn't smile and he only nodded instead of returning my hello. He followed me to the Service Counter. At the time I assumed he was there as a customer, but his presence made me uneasy. My face grew hot as customers and employees alike seemed to turn in my direction. I frantically asked to speak to the store's manager. I stood in front of the store's counter with Detective Kelsey standing closely behind me while I waited.

When the store manager appeared, I tried to lean in close to have a private conversation. He kept asking me to speak up. I raised my voice and began explaining to him my whole unfortunate ordeal involving the wire transactions made at the store. I noticed Detective Kelsey was still standing very closely behind me as I spoke to the store's manager. Once again I found myself giving a point-by-point rendition. I was emphatic that I had no inkling the money orders were counterfeit until after I had cashed them and wired all the money to Jessica.

Detective Kelsey stepped forward and said he needed to speak to me in the manager's office. I assumed he'd overheard and thought he could be of help. The three of us filed up the stairs and entered a small door. The wood paneled room was small, so much that the desk took up almost the entire available space. There were two chairs in front of the desk. The manager went to the chair closest to the corner and removed a stack of file folders and papers and added them to an existing pile on the edge of his desk. Kelsey said, "Start at the beginning." I explained everything once again while Kelsey took notes. He asked how Jessica and I met and how frequently I communicated with her through emails and telephone. He interrupted me and asked, "Do you have records of these conversations? Can you get me those chat room and email transcripts?" His request did not seem strange to me. If anything, this documentation would support my story. I had absolutely nothing to hide, so I agreed to give Detective Kelsey my full cooperation.

I returned back to my bank several days later. The bank official informed me that, as a result of the money orders being nonnegotiable, my checking account was now $5000 overdrawn. I tendered the $1000 leftover cash, and the bank gave me a credit line, which I used to pay back my remaining debt. I was embarrassed, but I was nevertheless relieved that the whole financial issue had been resolved, in spite of it leaving me in debt. Any possible crimes had been averted. I breathed a sigh of relief for the first time in weeks.

I returned to work the next day and discussed the embarrassing ordeal with my immediate supervisor, Cheryl. I explained that both Market Place Foods and my bank had been reimbursed. I vowed never again to commit myself to any online relationships. I told her, "The whole experience has left me leery not just of online romances, but also of conducting any online transactions. I much prefer face-to-face relationships and business transactions." She thanked me for keeping her in the loop, and we both returned to work.

One day about six months later, I was on duty driving the state vehicle making home visits to my clients when I received a call informing me that I had made the front headline news in the Sawyer County Record newspaper. The news of me being charged with these crimes hit me like a bolt of lightning. A sense of bewilderment suddenly engulfed my entire being. I pulled to the side of the road to collect my thoughts. What was going on? I needed confirmation. The first person I thought of was Rose. On the phone she confirmed the horrible news. I had been charged with nine counts of forgery and altering of US Postal money orders and was scheduled to appear in court on February 2nd to face those charges. These charges carried more than 15 years prison time if convicted. My heart dropped to the pit of my stomach. How could I be a member of law enforcement and not even know that I was charged with a crime, let alone that I was expected in court? All I could think about was my reputation in the community and how my employer and co-workers would now perceive me. Rose told me it was just a misunderstanding, but if it wasn't I needed a lawyer. Quick.

I finished my home visits and drove back to the office. When I walked in the door my supervisor was sitting at my desk. She told me that I was being placed on administrative leave with pay, effective immediately, and she notified me that she was launching an administrative investigation into the Sawyer County Record news reports pending the outcome of the prosecution against me in Sawyer County. I was too astounded to reply. She had already heard everything I had to say on the matter. How could this be happening? Was it all a misunderstanding and that's why no one told me personally about the charges?

This was real, and I needed help. I retained defense counsel, attorney Andrew Lawton. Prior to the initial court appearance, Mr. Lawton advised me that he had examined the prosecutor's criminal complaint and police reports that were filed, and he could find no evidence whatsoever implicating me in any crime. The only evidence the prosecutor had against me was based on hearsay from Detective Kelsey.

The night before the preliminary hearing, the entire town was frozen in sub-zero temperatures. I watched the snow outside my window as the most startling thought occurred to me: What if I can't get to the courthouse tomorrow? Could I go to jail for not showing up? I had been suffering from mental exhaustion since shortly after Jessica cursed me out and called me a thief. My job was at the center of all my plans for my future. I became convinced that the way to save my job was to clear myself of these charges. Dressed in warm layers and boots, I made my way to my vehicle, lifted the hood, and connected a battery charger to the car's battery to make sure it would start in the morning. Unlike my first trip out of Sierra Leone, or even my voyage through Europe to the US, I felt like this day, tomorrow, February 2, 2006, would be the day that mattered most in my life. I stayed up all night with my mind racing in anticipation of what I could expect to encounter the next day.

I arrived at the Sawyer County courthouse 45 minutes early and parked my car at the far end of the courthouse parking lot. I turned the engine off and sat there waiting. I sweated what felt like buckets of sweat in spite of the frozen cold temperatures. So this is how raw anxiety feels ... I took deep breaths with slow exhales trying to gather myself mentally. What I wouldn't have given for my mother's arms in that moment. I searched my mind for some sort of motivation to help me face the preliminary hearing. Thoughts of Tom's advice to serve God in all I do came to me. I asked myself what I had done wrong, and the answer that came to mind was that I fell in love. Who hasn't done that? I buttoned the top button on my coat, put my gloves back on my hands and walked through the courthouse doors with the last bit of fortitude in me. I soon find myself in the same courtroom where I'd once stood as a dignified and respectable member of law enforcement and conducted official state duty.

I took a seat on the bench outside the inner offices of the court. My attorney could see how nervous I was. He placed his hand on my shoulder for a moment then left me sitting there as he walked toward the prosecutor's office. He told me later that he'd gone to the prosecutor to insist that she drop all charges immediately if she wanted to avoid trial. He told me that she tried to persuade him to agree to a plea bargain.

I found out that Detective Kelsey told the court I had stated to him that I knew the money orders were bogus and counterfeit before I cashed them and wired the money to England. Why would he concoct such a lie? On both occasions I met with Detective Kelsey he advised me that my interviews with him were being voice recorded, although he could not produce a recording of my admission. The prosecutor could not provide a single substantive and collaborating piece of evidence. Why was I even in court? How did it get this far? I felt a deep sense of betrayal. How could my fellow law enforcement officials be so hell-bent on destroying me? I never imagined that my co-workers and neighbors would turn on me with such vengeance over a crime I was actually the victim of. I was sworn to uphold the laws of the State of Wisconsin and the Constitution of the United States. I took that pledge seriously, to the point that if I had committed a legitimate crime, I would have had no qualms or grievances against the prosecutor and the detective for coming after me.

Mr. Lawton and I reunited in the courtroom. It did not look anything like the courtrooms on television dramas. The judge sat behind a desk and my attorney and I sat at a long table, as did the prosecutor and his assistant. The court reporter was seated on a stool with a small stenograph machine in front of her. The prosecutor's words sounded jumbled in my ears. I felt afloat and flushed down a drain. She seemed to go on forever. I was jarred out of my haze by Mr. Lawton clearing his throat and pushing his chair away from the table. He told the court that if there was a crime committed in this case, then it had been committed against me. I drifted into my thoughts. I went over the minutiae of what happened. I asked God why he had allowed me to meet and fall in love with Jessica. With a hammer of the gavel the session was over. I had not understood what had just transpired, as I was overwhelmed and consumed by it all. I felt as though the reality that was familiar had been replaced by a somehow alien one.

My attorney instructed me on what I had to do as a result of the morning's proceeding. Booked? As in arrested? I couldn't believe what I was hearing. I was unable to clear my mind of anything besides what I had to do in response to these unfounded allegations. How could I work in law enforcement with an arrest record? I kept wondering, *What do these people want from me?*

That afternoon I found myself in a familiar place—the county jail, a place where I had once taken offenders into custody. Knowing and being known by all of the officers made being fingerprinted a humiliating, tortuous experience. When I stepped to the counter, Officer Peterson opened the fingerprinting device, and I extended my hand. Two other officers came to stand nearby and observe the process. Officer Peterson grabbed my fingers and looked at me, shaking his head. I heard the other officers snicker. The walk of shame from the fingerprinting area to the wall where my mug shot would be taken was a trip I never imagined I'd take, in my wildest dreams. Officer Peterson did not utter a word to me, but his eyes and body language suggested that he was sympathetic to my situation. He had always been quite friendly to me when I came to the jail to conduct official state business. I left the Sawyer County Jail humiliated and disgusted. How dare these people do this to me? This was my life they were toying with.

I called my attorney later that afternoon, both to report that I had been through processing and to ask about the next step in the process. He told me that the next proceeding would be a scheduling conference on June 12th. Four months away. I just wanted it to be over. Mr. Lawton went over again what had happened in the courtroom earlier that day to make certain that I understood everything. I had been walking around feeling like I had gotten kicked in the head since the whole ordeal began.

As I waited for the next court hearing I had to contend with the administrative inquiry from my employer. The inquiry required me to comply with all investigatory interrogations; I answered endless questions during the investigatory inquisition, and nothing was sacred. They pried into my love life and interviewed everyone on my caseload, looking for damning evidence. I was fighting to hold onto my life and my dignity, and convinced that I had broken no law, I began to look forward to the day that a jury of my peers would decide my fate.

As the only professional black male in the area, I was visible at all times, and I constantly encountered offenders in my case load in the community. I repeatedly heard that they had been told I no longer worked for the department because of the criminal charges against me. At the time, the investigation that would determine my employment status had not been concluded. I wondered why my co-workers would spread information that was untrue.

There was no presumption of innocence in the process; instead, the system appeared to assume I was guilty unless proven otherwise. I began to rack my brain for clues to how I had ended up in this place. Did my urgent move to Hayward to be closer to Tom's mother cause me to fail to recognize the disdain and discontent my co-workers had against me? Was I so mesmerized by the beauty of Sawyer County that I completely overlooked my colleagues' subtle and unwelcoming overtures? Had I been naïve to assume that my white co-workers would accept me into their community with open arms in the first place? These and other questions and doubts continued to puzzle me as I struggled for clues as to why my co-workers turned against me.

I was now fighting the charges in circuit court as well as my employer's inquiry with my entire spirit and soul. Most days I felt like I was bent backwards over a barrel, overextended to the point of powerlessness. I was at my wit's end, and I knew that Jesus Christ was not coming down from Heaven to do the footwork for me. My prayer life had always helped me maintain balance, so I continued attending the Baptist church with Virginia twice a month.

One day, after running into a client who had been told I no longer worked for the department, I sat in my car for a long time thinking about how unfair the whole situation was. I prayed, asking God for direction. *Why do they talk about me as if I'm not still here? Are dignity and hubris the same thing? How can I bear the weight, Lord? Haven't I been a humble servant? Haven't I let your will abide in my life? Tell me what to do now, Father.* I resolved in that moment to once again place my entire fate into the hands of my higher power, Lord God Jesus Christ. I committed my entire being—mental, spiritual and physical—to God.

I was alone up against a big and powerful bureaucratic governmental entity that had unlimited resources. The emotional stability I needed to withstand the protracted legal proceedings required me to devise and implement a survival mechanism. In order to develop and maintain a positive attitude—gratitude, appreciation, enthusiasm, confidence, humility and, most importantly, forgiveness—I became mindful about my sleep, nutrition and exercise routines. I jog for miles every day. I joined the Northwoods Fitness Center and the fitness center at the Holiday Inn in Saint Croix Falls. I could focus on my health and get results, and live to fight another day.

Summer came quickly. On June 12th the prosecutor told the court that all charges against me were dismissed on prosecutor's motion. I felt Mr. Lawton embrace my shoulder, but I was unable to move. I was frozen in my chair, but I felt as though a gigantic weight had been lifted off my shoulders, and that was quickly followed by a feeling of euphoria. I felt as if I could fly. Plans for the future flooded my mind. A smile spread across my face, and no matter how hard I tried I could not make it go away. That night I went to the Snowshoe Bar and toasted to my victory.

The relief I felt from being exonerated was short-lived. I was quite baffled to learn that the prosecutor had covertly prepared a deferred prosecution agreement without the consent and approval of my attorney and submitted these legal documents to the court, where they were signed by the judge. The prosecutor's secret, ex-parte document made it appear in official court records that I had admitted to committing theft of check crime and that I had agreed to a deferred prosecution agreement with the District Attorney's office for one year, during which time I agreed to pay restitution and to commit no crime. My employer, who at the time was looking for any legitimate reason to terminate my employment, would have found the prosecutor's illegal document and used it as a pretext to terminate my employment.

I had thought the whole awful mess was over. What vindictiveness. Why was the prosecutor bent on my demise? My attorney assured me the illegal measure would not stand. He immediately drafted a letter to the judge expressing his outright disappointment, indignation and disgust at the prosecutor's blatant violations of rules of professional conduct. Reluctantly, the prosecutor submitted her amended motion to dismiss to the court. With my final exoneration in hand and documented in official court records, I returned to work.

One evening I sat in the Snowshoe Bar talking to the bartender. He asked, "Why so down? I heard your legal troubles went away."

"Johnny, I just can't figure it out. How did it all come to this? Court and everything? I know these people from work. If someone told me that one of the guys I worked with was involved in some riff-raff I would give the guy the benefit of the doubt. No. They pick on me, try to get me fired and thrown in prison. What went wrong?"

Johnny was drying a pilsner glass with a bar towel. His lips parted as if he was about to say something, then he closed his mouth, shook his head and started to walk to the other end of the bar.

"What?" I cried.

Johnny placed the glass on the rack behind the bar and flipped the towel onto his shoulder. He put his hands on the bar and leaned forward. "Are you serious?" he asked, jutting his chin forward. I must have looked puzzled, so he continued. "Frank, you aren't white. Those people never really accepted you as their co-worker. They just tolerated you until they saw an opportunity to get rid of you."

It was my turn. "Are you serious?" I said. There was no way I could accept that all my work relationships had been fake. And because I was black? "That's not how it works," I said.

He cut me off saying, "You mark my words. If you were white they never would have put you through the ringer the way they did. What went wrong is that you were born black and chose to live in America. You want another beer, Frank?"

I was in shock. I thought back to how people in Algeria treated darker-skinned Africans differently from the fair-skinned Muslims. Could this be? According to Johnny's explanation, nothing that I did mattered. I had been a good employee, and I tendered compassionate service to all my clients. Who cares if I'm not white? My stomach began to turn, and I lost my desire to sit in the bar.

Again I thought the whole sordid mess was over, but next came my civil rights battle in federal court against my employer. Looking back, I guess I was naïve to think that I had settled in Hayward for good, and could return to work without any problems.

At work I was blatantly and relentlessly mistreated and held to unequal terms and conditions of employment by my immediate supervisor. The discrimination I endured in Hayward reached its peak when my supervisor accused me of losing my financial booklet. When I replied that I had not lost it, but had sent the booklet to him earlier, he clinched his fist, pounded the desk, and pointed his finger at me, saying, "Get out of my office, and go back to Africa." With that, the arbitrator overturned all my suspensions and ordered that I receive my back pay. He further ruled that my investigations and suspensions had been unwarranted and were motivated by race.

The EEOC also investigated my grievances and found my employer had violated the Civil Rights Act of 1964, which prompted me to file a discrimination lawsuit in the US District court in Milwaukee.

What I needed was a place where I belonged. I decided to get away from the protracted painful litigation while the process ground on and visit Assini, Greece because it was the first home I'd made away from Africa on my own.

My December 2008 visit to Greece came immediately after the unfortunate incident during which Greek police shot and killed fifteen-year-old Alexanderos Girgoropoulos in Athens. The incident sparked massive demonstrations and riots in Athens. In the aftermath of the riots in and around the Syntagma Square, I saw broken windows and charred buildings.

Athens had changed tremendously since 1983. The city had succumbed to European capitalistic influence as evidenced by new shopping outlets, car dealerships and gas stations. Additionally, the presence of tourists from all over the world was undeniable. When I'd lived in Greece in the 1980s, the majority of visible foreigners were European and American tourists. Now there were numerous Pakistanis, Indians, Africans, Iraqis, Syrians, Jordanians, Eastern Europeans, and numerous kinds of gypsies from around Europe.

Athens was so highly congested that I immediately took the bus to Nafplio and eventually on to Assini. I noticed the countryside hadn't changed much. However, as we approached Argos, I began to notice the heavy presence of European influence. The landscape changed. What had once been orange and olive farms were now highly developed areas with modern European car dealerships and European style homes. In Nafplio, I noticed several modern gas stations and appliances stores and designer clothing stores. I began to feel nervous in the face of all the changes, but much to my delight, the bus station at the foothills of the castle overlooking Nafplio still looked the same. But the post office had been replaced by a tourist attraction site, and I noticed several restaurants and souvenir shops. On the way to Assini I saw another European car dealership and noticed several new American made vehicles on the car lot.

On the bus I fantasized about reunions with old friends in Assini. I wondered if there would be any familiar faces. I was looking forward to visiting the orange farms I helped to establish, and wondered if they would they still be there or could they have been turned into a subdivision as well? I couldn't wait to sit inside the Takis Café where I'd once acted as a job broker between my European friends and Greek farmers. A funny thought occurred to me: What if my old friends think I'm here looking for work? I laughed out loud at this thought. The fellow in the seat in front of mine sat up and turned around to look at me. I kept laughing and waved him on.

I finally arrived in Assini at night, and spent the night in a hotel in Tolon. I was disappointed at what I saw the next morning when I walked out of my hotel. There were no more public beaches; the wide, extensive beach now had a wall erected for privacy, and access to the beach was limited to use by the beachfront hotels. I was deeply disturbed by this. A young American tourist explained that it was political. Private beaches were one of the effects of privatization of public lands and services. I could not believe my ears.

I arrived at my final destination the next day: the Café Takis in Assini. I sat down and waited to see if I could recognize anyone from 1983, or perhaps if someone would recognize me. I saw no familiar faces. There were no European vagabonds to be found. Even though Café Takis looked the same, the entire culture of the place had changed. An old Greek man walked by my table, so I got up and followed him. When I got his attention, he looked at me with surprise and excitement. He blurted out loud "malakas" in a jubilant tone. I had forgotten his name, but he had not forgotten my face. He reminded me that his name was Yannis.

He recognized me because I had worked for his father, Demetris. He was so elated to see me that he grabbed me by the hand and took me to a café where he knew people would recognize me. As soon as we entered the café Yannis blurted out "malakas" again, which is an expletive often used by Greeks as a friendly greeting. Several old Greek men, busy playing dominoes and drinking coffee, recognized me. I sat down among them. Though I had lost virtually all my Greek, I did manage to utter a word here and there. I managed to explain that I was not in Assini looking for work. The men laughed and one of them said, "You are too old to hop a tree like you used to."

I thought about what he said. I couldn't express it in Greek, but I was in the best shape of my life and could've hopped an orange tree with no problem. I didn't want to pick fruit because I was on vacation. I wondered if these men had a concept of vacation. The Greek agrarian work ethic doesn't leave a lot of room for leisure. I abandoned my thoughts about the cultural differences between my now American sensibility and their old-fashioned Greek ways. I lifted my glass and toasted, "To the oranges." We laughed and talked in broken Greek and English.

An old lady walked into the café and when she recognized me she screamed out loud with excitement. The woman's name was Marina, and she and her husband Aristides owned a grocery store and several acres of orange and olive plantations. I had worked for Aristides numerous times doing a variety of jobs. When I mentioned his name Marina cried and told me that Aristides had passed away years ago. I put my arm around her shoulder as she wept and said a silent prayer for Aristides' eternal soul. Marina soon dried her face with her apron and slipped her arm around my waist. She squeezed me tight with one arm and said, "Welcome home."

Word quickly went around the village about my presence. Yorogos Christopolos-Vangelis walked into the café—the man who had let me live in his farm house on the orange fields. Yorogos was excited to see me. I was delighted to be able to have this experience, to see these people again after so many years. Yorogos took me around his farms where I had once worked picking oranges, mandarins, olives and apricots. I spent the rest of the day in Assini in the cafés catching up with old friends.

I ventured back to Nafplio. I met up in a restaurant with a group of friendly and educated Greek men who spoke perfect English. Our friendly discussion soon evolved into a lively political debate. The way out of Greece's economic crisis was a highly divisive topic, and the debate among the Greeks themselves was passionate. One man smiled broadly as he insisted that Greece should remain a part of the European Community and that austerity, as painful as it was, would provide the temporary fiscal discipline Greece needed in order to move forward. Another man wore a scowl and beat the table, explaining that the once generous social programs and benefits were being wiped out at the expense of the poor workers. He insisted that the result of the austerity measures would be that more Greeks would be worse off. A younger man chimed in, arguing that Europe was imposing its capitalistic and materialistic values onto Greece and that the only beneficiaries of Greece remaining in the European Community and implementing austerity measures would be the large banks.

I was delighted to be privy to such a lively discussion. I was reminded of the many nights that my friends would gather at my farm house on Yorogos' land. We would roast oranges, drink, and talk about everything from creation to life after death. Then and now, this type of socializing nourished my mind and made me feel connected to the people around me.

My goodbyes in Greece were as warm as the greetings I had received. Marina gave me a jar of honey to take home with me, and Yorogos met me at the café for one last beer. I left Greece feeling reinvigorated. I could see my value in the eyes of every person I spent time with. I had begun to relax again.

I went back to work upon my return from Greece. My work environment was still quite tense, but memories of my beautiful vacation in Assini helped me manage my daily challenges. My lawsuit against my employer for discrimination and harassment was still pending and I was anxious for it to end. My attorney, Mr. Kurt Kobelt, a reputable civil rights lawyer told me that the state had filed a series of motions in an attempt to dismiss the case, which had held up setting a court date. Judge Adelman rejected all of the state's motions and the court allowed my lawsuit to move forward to trial.

My employer agreed to settle the case for $80,000 inclusive of attorney's fees and costs, agreed to refrain from retaliation against me for my lawsuits, agreed to other terms and conditions, and I kept my job. Finally, I thought, it was all over.

In December of 2009, I returned home to Sierra Leone for the first time since 1991. I knew my country had gone through a brutal and savage war, during which rebels took over the diamond mines in the Kono District, kidnapping and raping women and recruiting child soldiers who carried out the most heinous of crimes. Rebels captured and established strongholds in important diamond mining towns. I watched the media coverage of the war and had a terrible feeling deep in my heart that my village of Punduru would bear the brunt of the violence. Unfortunately, my prediction turned out to be correct.

My village had been completely devastated by the rebels. One night, as they crossed the Sewa River on their way to the Kono District region, and while the people in my village slept, the rebels threw grenades into the houses, setting them all ablaze and wiping out entire sections of the village. My sister Bettie told me that our house had been the first one the rebels torched, as it was the first house standing on the hill on the way to Jaiama Sewafe. Luckily my family had managed to escape into the bushes behind the house. With the exception of an elderly woman I knew named Mama-Baindu who perished in the fires, the entire village escaped the carnage and spent the next 10 years in the bushes hiding from rebels.

As I stood and gazed at the wreckage, at the barren landscape of my Punduru, the carnage unleashed a venomous rage in me. I asked God, *what did my people do to deserve to be attacked and have their homes burnt? Is this your will?* The gravity of the devastation pulled heavily on my mind. I sank down into a squat near the skeleton of what had once been our vibrant orange tree and wept. I stayed there until almost dark. I resolved that something good would grow out of the ashes of Punduru.

The next day I visited the towns of Yengema and Koidu. I was devastated at what I saw. Rusted heavy mining equipment was strewn around. The NDMC administrative headquarters had been reduced to rubble. In both towns the buildings had been torn down and reduced to ruins. Bandits had torn down the once luxurious homes at the bungalows. There was diesel oil all over the land. Bandits had dug for diamonds everywhere, even in the middle of road. The former NDMC airport had a large pit dug out in the middle of the runway.

The Kono District remains richly endowed with significant amounts of diamond deposits, as evidenced by the continued mining operations. Long after the demise of NDMC and the cessation of rebel assaults and takeover of the mines, the region still attracted foreign investors, as is evidenced by the foreign mining operations in Koidu. Unfortunately, these foreign companies continue to steal from our people.

As I reflected on the failure of our political leaders, I became even more grateful to Thomas Johnson for having changed my life. There were many other poor African children he could have encountered that day, yet God chose me. Without Tom's altruistic nature and generosity, I am not certain what my life would look like. There would probably not have been any secondary school, college or graduate school. There probably would have been no time in Ghana, Italy, or Greece. And there would probably have been no Saturday evenings and Sunday mornings with Virginia Johnson, and no Ojibwa friends. The fact is that I had few chances based on where I was born, and Tom changed the odds for me.

I spent the remainder of my time in Sierra Leone trying to enjoy the natural wonders. One day I saw a flyer for a safari hunt. "Genuine Real Wild African Animals," it said. For a split second I considered going, and in that moment I missed Gaby. I knew that my time in Africa was meant for me to rediscover my roots. I found a land and its resilient people determined to survive. I felt that God had seen fit to show me my country in a moment in my life when I needed to understand who I was and where I had come from. I was thankful for the chance to reunite with my sisters and their grown children. I learned of other family members who had made the journey to America, too. I felt that my return home helped solidify my view of myself and my value as a person. I bid a tearful goodbye to my family and returned to my life in Milwaukee.

Each time I enter the United States I picture the Statute of Liberty welcoming me to America. To my mind this gift from the French to the American people commemorates both the French and American revolutions and symbolizes the democratic ideals of freedom, equality, liberty and fraternity. This particular time that I returned to the United States, I tried to picture what each of these ideals might look like in my life. I wondered what the future held.

The gruesome and protracted civil rights litigation was behind me and I had kept my job. I returned hopeful for a future with the department, and on more than one occasion I envisioned myself staying there until retirement.

Six months after I returned from Sierra Leone, I found myself back in federal court for the same behaviors I had sued my employer over. My immediate supervisors had intentionally violated the terms and conditions of the settlement agreement by retaliating against me through a series of workplace harassments, intimidations and humiliations, during which I was verbally abused. This created a hostile work environment for me. The EEOC once again investigated my charge, found probable cause of violations, and granted me the right to sue in federal court.

It was during my second lawsuit litigation in 2014 that I learned of several damning email correspondences between state officials and Hayward PD regarding my wrongful prosecution in Sawyer County some 10 years prior. These emails were never intended to be made public, and had been discovered in 2006 by my attorneys during my first lawsuit against my employer. I was never told about them because they were criminal matters and not relevant to the civil claims that were at issue before the court. During my second lawsuit, I was required to provide my attorney with the complete case file from the first lawsuit, so I drove from Milwaukee to Madison to pick it up from my previous attorneys. Among the materials I discovered a folder labeled, "criminal investigation," and in it were several email correspondences and messages written by my employer referencing conversations with Hayward PD and the Sawyer County prosecutor's office regarding my prosecution in Hayward.

One such email was written by a regional chief to the administrator, copying several state officials who were in direct contact with the Hayward PD and Sawyer County prosecutor. The chief wrote that he had met with FBI officials in Eau Claire and advised them that I may be linked to international terrorism involving the bombing in England. He implored them to investigate and charge me with federal crimes involving US postal money orders. The email further stated that the FBI officials told him I was not linked to terrorism and that I had been a victim of an Internet scam.

When I first saw these emails in 2014, I was deeply disturbed by the lengths that these people had gone to in order to persecute me. I even wondered if I should be concerned for my safety. Why were they so hellbent to destroy me? And why had they ignored and disregarded the advice of the FBI and proceeded with my wrongful prosecution? After all, I had beaten them at their game three times over. I resolved to stand my ground. The way these people had treated me over the years was inexcusable.

June 3, 2014 was a day of reckoning for me. My fate was held in the balance inside a federal courtroom. The settlement agreement conference for my second civil rights lawsuit was held before the Honorable Judge Lynn Adelman. I knew I had strong case, but I also knew my attorney was more interested in settling the case, as she lacked the resources to take the case to trial.

Weeks before the settlement date, my attorney had advised me that the State was insisting that any settlement must include my resignation. I knew if the union were still viable and intact at the workplace, under no circumstances would the State demand I forfeit my employment. In my first lawsuit the union supported me during litigation; this time I had no such backing. The absence of union representation at the workplace has left public workers in Wisconsin severely demoralized.

In the days before the settlement conference, my lawyer and I got into a heated debate over the amount I considered reasonable under the circumstance of being required to forfeit my job. I found myself in a very difficult situation. I believed that the State had the upper hand in the negotiations because of the absence of the union. I had built a life around my identity as a probation and parole agent. Who would I become? Every time I'd try to picture myself doing something else for a living, living someplace other than Wisconsin, I drew a complete blank. Thinking about my professional future brought on an anxiety that felt like a block of ice in my gut. The chill made it hard to breathe. I was afraid that I was going to lose my representation, so I relented and reluctantly agreed to begin settlement talks with a $200,000 offer. Of course I knew that the State would never pay that amount.

The night before the conference I didn't sleep well. I had a good job, and losing it for no reason, when in fact I was the victim, was extremely hard to accept. Moreover, the entire situation would make it extremely difficult to find a similar job. Bullies had invaded my work space and the only thing I had done was to call them out for their bad acts. I had only wished to be left alone to do my job, one for which I was well qualified. My American dream had centered on the acquisition of education, experience and skills. Why wasn't the formula working?

Leaving my job of over 13 years felt like punishment. Throughout my legal fight to hold on to my job, I regularly sought spiritual guidance and strength from my pastor at Saint Martin de Porres Catholic parish. A few days before the conference, my pastor and I joined hands and prayed that justice be done. I continued praying: *Heavenly Father, Lord of Mercy. I have no wrath. Vengeance is yours. I ask where is the justice in the wake of the havoc that these people have wreaked in my life? Spread your grace on me, Lord. Touch the hearts of all concerned and see that justice is served in this case. I thank you for your loving-kindness and your tender mercy which is so often visited upon me.*

The morning of the conference I boarded the bus headed for downtown Milwaukee to the federal courthouse with justice on my mind. I had decided to fight with every fiber of my being. As I took my seat I felt a sudden excitement, and for a moment I almost forgot my fears and anxiety. I became excited because I realized I would soon be meeting Judge Adelman. I had been told by my previous and current attorneys that Judge Adelman was a good judge and that he was sympathetic to plaintiffs in civil rights discrimination cases. In fact, just a few months earlier Judge Adelman had made national headlines when he struck down the unpopular Wisconsin Voter ID law as unfair and discriminatory. I was hopeful that Judge Adelman would be a champion for justice.

I got off the bus and walked up the steps at the federal courthouse. After passing through security I was directed to Judge Adelman's courtroom. I met my attorneys in the lobby and we sat in silence. I remember looking at my attorney and thinking, *Is there anything I can say to her that will help save my job?* A part of me wanted to continue fighting, but the reality was that I was mentally exhausted and financially drained.

I entered the courtroom with my attorneys and the clerk directed us to the law library, where we waited for Judge Adelman. Shortly afterwards the judge walked in and said hello to all of us. I noticed he had a yellow pad in his hand. He directed us into his spacious courtroom. I told him as I walked past that it was an honor and a privilege to meet him. He smiled and nodded.

The room radiated an aura of power and solemnity. The courtroom was silent. There were no marshals or court reporters, just the thick blue carpeting and the polished mahogany chairs and tables. The judge's bench was raised up and positioned in such a way that it hovered over his entire courtroom. An enormous painting of President John F. Kennedy hung on the wall directly facing the judge's bench.

Judge Adelman walked around the large table and sat directly opposite me. I had brought two liters of bottled water with me because I knew Judge Adelman expected to hear directly from me, and this made me somewhat nervous. My lawyer spoke very briefly and the judge began to ask me questions. I maintained direct eye contact with him, and I managed to plead my case. After explaining all that had happened, I also told him I very much desired to keep my job in spite of all the injustices I had endured over the years at the hands of state officials. I felt oddly empowered. I told the judge that it was unfair of the state to demand I resign from my job, because I had been the victim. I pleaded to Judge Adelman that as a black man my age I would face extremely difficult times finding a similar job, especially with a record of having successfully sued a state agency twice.

Judge Adelman was listening carefully. He maintained eye contact until he glanced down and tore off a single page from the yellow pad in front of him on the mahogany table. He folded the page in half and made notations. I paused while he was writing. The judge waited patiently to see if I was going to continue speaking, but I remained silent. Judge Adelman finally said, "Well, I am just the messenger." He got up and walked to the adjacent conference room where the State of Wisconsin lawyers and officials were waiting for him.

Judge Adelman spent about fifteen minutes with them. He returned to the courtroom and again sat opposite me. He said, "They want you gone, Mr. Mandewah. I threw out the figure of $200,000 to settle the case, but they rejected that outright."

My world came tumbling down as I sat facing the judge and absorbing his comments. The State wanted me gone? They were really demanding my resignation? This was happening. What would I do for work? Should I stay in Wisconsin? I couldn't go back to living in Greece. I wished that Tom were around; somehow I felt like he would help make this right. I thought of myself old and trying to pick fruit, and I felt like laughing. Then I was once again angry. I took a deep breath and chose my words carefully.

Once again I told the judge that I very much wanted my job, and that I was a victim and being forced out through no fault of my own. I concluded that I felt $150,000 would be a reasonable alternative, considering I was losing my job.

The judge went back to the State officials for further conversations and when he returned, Judge Adelman told me that the State was willing to consider a six month severance package at my regular salary along with $50,000 inclusive of attorney's fees and costs.

When I continued pleading my case, my attorney interrupted and blurted out that she would withdraw from the case if I did not accept the state's settlement offer. It was a real conundrum. I truly felt I had been hung out to dry by my own lawyer. I either had to agree or start all over again. I sat with my head in my hands trying to resolve the problem. Should I retain another attorney? How long, in fact, could I go on? I felt that the deck was stacked against me.

I summed it up in my mind. I had been fighting constantly for ten years, and I had to face the fact that I did not or could not match the resources of the State bureaucracy. I felt that as an immigrant I had no chance when trying to stand up against a powerful and entrenched system.

By now, everyone in the courtroom was waiting for me to recompose myself and deliver my response. The room was silent. I couldn't just kept sitting and contemplating, leaving a renowned federal judge waiting for my decision.

Finally I raised my head from my palms and looked at Judge Adelman and said, "Judge Adelman, I agree to the State's offer. I am exhausted from this fight to hold onto my job. I have been fighting for ten years, and I can go no further."

Afterwards, I continued to speak to the judge. I told him that as an immigrant I was still grateful to be here in spite of what I had endured at the hands of the Wisconsin Department of Corrections. I told him that a white man had given me an opportunity to be in America, and now it was a white man who took away the same opportunity because of my race.

I told the judge how I met Tom Johnson and how he subsequently brought me to the United States. I told him about my origins of extreme poverty and my life of hardship. I noticed the interest in the judge's eyes as he listened to my story. I knew he was liberal and thus sympathetic to me, and also that he was a champion for civil rights, so I knew he had been fair. I also knew that he was somewhat constricted in his authority and ability to allow me to keep my job if the State of Wisconsin was so strongly against my keeping it.

Finally we all gathered in the courtroom and Judge Adelman took his position on the bench. The court was called into session. I saw the court reporter and the clerk take their places. The structure of Judge Adelman's court was such that the plaintiff and his attorneys occupied the front row seat and the defendants and their attorneys occupied the back seat. I turned around and looked at the State officials while Judge Adelman spoke. When the judge asked me if I had anything to say I responded that I was truly disgusted with the decisions of the State officials.

This time, the fall of the gavel gave me nothing to celebrate. I felt that I had been stripped of my dignity and set back thirteen years in my professional career. It was, in a word, unfair. The agreement that was brokered in the second lawsuit settlement barred me from ever seeking employment with the State of Wisconsin, its agencies and/or its affiliates. I took this to mean that they wanted me out of Wisconsin. I reasoned that I was due for a change of scenery anyway; the winters in Wisconsin were far too cold.

Indeed Hayward had become a paradox to me; it was a place where I had once felt that I was experiencing my long-envisioned American dream, and it was a place that left me with overwhelming strife, betrayal, and bitter memories. Long after my innocence had been established I was still grappling with doubt and ambivalence at my inexplicable persecution. Between the years 2004 and 2014, I saw my self-worth blossom, disintegrate, and prepare to be reborn.

Chapter 19

PRIOR TO STARTING my job with the State of Wisconsin I hadn't given much thought to my self-worth. I had been a good son, brother and friend, but I had also been a poor student and a failure at marriage. So when I first felt the deep sense of satisfaction that accompanies meaningful work, I reasoned that my performance at my job was a good indicator of the quality of human being I was. With every day I felt my sense of self grow and take further root. The relentless attacks on my character by my employer, losing my job, and the pursuit by the police and the prosecutor left me feeling hollow.

Though she was the person I felt closest to, I chose not to tell Tom's mother what I was going through in Hayward, or that criminal prosecution had turned my life into a rollercoaster ride. Virginia had become like a mother to me, and I was embarrassed and ashamed that I found myself in the midst of trouble. She was in her early eighties, and I didn't want to upset her or have her worry for me. She had done so much for me for so long. I could not risk pushing her away.

Whenever I visited her I slept in Tom's bedroom, which had been reserved for visits from him and his family. One weekend she told me to look through Tom's belongings and take whatever I wanted. I found Tom's flight logs, beginning when he came home from Vietnam. The logs held all the information regarding Tom's career, right down to the particulars of each flight. I also found an Award of Distinguished Flying Cross that Tom was issued by the United States Army for his heroism while participating in aerial flights evidenced by voluntary action above and beyond the call of duty in the Republic of Vietnam. He'd told me he was shot down in Vietnam. He even showed me the scar on his knee from the bullet that went through his leg, but Tom never mentioned the award. My discoveries simply confirmed what I already knew: Tom was not a boastful person, but rather a simple, humble man. In fact Tom's uncle's wife once said to me that Tom was an extremely meek and humble person.

My discovery of Tom's award made Memorial Day services even more special for us. In 2005, Virginia and I went to the cemetery in Milaca, where Memorial Day is graciously celebrated. The entire town gathers at the cemetery as a marching band plays and the veterans, in full uniform, march. When the parade ends the people gather at the edge of the cemetery across the Rum River. They sit in rows of folding chairs and on the grass, while the veterans perform the annual rituals, including calling out the names of all the deceased veterans. That year I felt a special sense of anticipation. Tom deserved some credit, and in this small way he was being rightfully acknowledged, not just for risking his life in Vietnam but for giving his life in service to God every day. I sat beside Virginia and attentively waited. When I heard the name "Thomas Johnson" I rose and said, "Yes," before taking my seat once again. I felt connected to Tom, sitting there with his mother, thanking him for service beyond compare on and off the battlefield.

Tom's mother eventually moved to the Elam Nursing Home a block away from her home. The staff there became aware of our special relationship. At first I could see the curiosity in their eyes: why does this black man come to visit this old white woman? Virginia seemed to be unaware of the nurses' curiosity, and she lit up with joy each time I visited her. I carried a deep sense of duty to her, and she was such a compassionate person that just being around her lifted my spirits even in the worst of times.

When I visited her during the summer months, I'd take her out in her wheelchair for a stroll along the sidewalk. I'd find us a nice bench, with a bit of shade from a tree, and we'd stop. I secured her wheelchair directly facing me, with her back to the sun and we passed the afternoons with casual conversation. I listened with great interest when Virginia told me about her family lineage. She was born Virginia Elizabeth Pond in a house that her

missionary grandparents built in Bloomington. Her other relatives Samuel
Wilson Pond and Gideon Hollister Pond, were two missionary bothers
who came from Connecticut to built the first church in Bloomington—Oak
Grove Presbyterian Church. The brothers worked with the Dakota Indians
developing and translating their language and established themselves in the
area. The Gideon Pond House in Minneapolis is preserved today as a historical site and is included in the Historical Society of the State of
Minnesota.

Once Virginia said, "I must convert you to a Republican before I die."

"Mother Johnson, I'm a Democrat. Why would I want to change?" I
said. A pigeon came over to the bench, pecking the ground near my feet. I
laughed and said, "I thought we put this issue to bed with that Baptist talk.
Too bad we don't have any bread for the birds."

"Don't try and change the subject, Francis. There will be plenty of
birds to feed when we've finished talking. Now listen to me," she said as
she patted her knees with her hands.

I studied the swollen, arthritic joints on her fingers. Her skin was so
thin as to be transparent, and I could trace the purple veins from the back
of her hands all the way up her arms with my eyes. I grasped one of her
small, warm hands and pressed it against my cheek and said, "I'm listening."

"Good boy. Now vote Republican. You understand?" she said, allow-
ing me to caress my face with her hand.

"Mother, could you love a Catholic Democrat?"

"Francis, you are incorrigible." She pulled her hand from my grip. "I
suppose I have been loving a Democrat all this time. All my boys … did
Tom know you were a Democrat, of all things?"

"I don't know. Tom and I didn't talk a lot about American politics.
You know, Mother, no one has ever blessed me more than Tom and you. I
thank you."

"I know, dear Tom was such a good boy, and you, look at you." She
leaned forward in her wheelchair and placed one hand in mine and patted
my cheek with her free hand. "You've come so far. God blesses us when
the time comes. Simple servants like me and Tom are powerless to do anything but love you. You are a good man, Francis, because God made you
that way. I'm so proud of you."

A tear rolled down my cheek. I hoped that what she was saying was true. God made me what I am, and God had blessed me. This idea renewed my hope. When the time comes, God would be there for me like he always had been. Virginia began to hum a tune I couldn't recognize, and soon we were both swaying with the rhythm of her humming. We sat there in the quiet of the afternoon, enjoying each other's company for hours.

When Virginia fell ill, I spent even more time at the nursing home. One day I was just about to walk out the door to my car when a gentleman walked through the door. We made eye contact, and he said, "Are you Francis?" I held his gaze for a few seconds, studying his height and facial features. I looked deep into his eyes and saw something familiar. "Yes. Are you Tom's brother?"

"Yes, I'm Doug. The doctor just diagnosed her with Lou Gehrig's disease. It's incurable, and she doesn't have long before the disease takes over."

Doug's words knocked the wind out of me. I sat down in the waiting area and cradled my face in my hands. I lifted my head and asked, "What happens when the disease takes over? Will she be in pain?" Doug walked over to me, placed his hand on my shoulder and sat down beside me. "I know it's hard. She won't have any control over her body, but she shouldn't be in pain. The doctors will make her comfortable."

My thoughts were scattered. I thought about what my life would be like without her. I was moved to tears at the thought of empty Sunday mornings at church without her. I entertained some self-pity, asking God, *Why this mother, too?*

The months following were tense. The one person I had been able to count on over the years was now facing death. I struggled to not make Virginia's illness about me, but I couldn't help feeling like I needed her in my life and therefore her impending death was unfair. I prayed for her health constantly, asking God to limit her suffering and reveal a cure.

I received multiple calls from the head nurse, because it looked like the end of Virginia's natural life was at hand. But Virginia kept holding on, day in and day out. She grew disoriented and unresponsive. When I would enter her room I would be met with a blank stare. She and I would maintain eye contact without any speech. During these periods I would remember the times I'd visit and she would smile and greet me with open arms. Now she just lay there. Doug's wife, Diane, had brought music, but I didn't know if Virginia was hearing it.

I still remember the last time I spent with Virginia: she lay quietly in bed while I sat at her bedside holding her hand. I kept praying for her to utter a single word. "Sit up and try to convert me. Talk to me about last week's Sunday school lesson. Anything, Mother. Just say something," I said, but my pleas went unanswered. I choked back tears and passed the afternoon in the still of Virginia's room with Mozart's "Piano Sonata" drifting in the air.

Two days later Doug left a message that Virginia had passed. She was interred in the Forest Hills Cemetery next to her husband and close to Tom.

I visited the cemetery to pay my respects to Tom and Virginia. I spoke quietly to her again, explaining how sorry I was to have kept a secret from her. I imagined her in Heaven, an angel with God, all knowing. As I weeded the graves of the Johnson family it occurred to me how truly powerless I was. Perhaps that's what Mother Johnson had meant when she said all she could do was love me. I felt a pang in my heart. I felt like I was 15 again, watching Tom drive away from my school headed out of Sierra Leone. I felt utterly alone. In that moment my mind drifted to the legal troubles I was battling at the time. What does it mean to be completely powerless when an opponent with vast power and resources has singled you out? I came to the conclusion that it means God is in control.

With Tom, my mother, and Virginia gone, I felt alone in the world. It was difficult to muster the strength to continue the fight. Was I really innocent? Did I deserve to lose my job? Did I deserve to go to jail? Was I of irredeemable character? I had never entertained these sorts of questions before.

When the end of my 10-year nightmare came, and I lost my job and was barred from employment by the State of Wisconsin, I knew I needed to get out of Wisconsin immediately, before the bullies come after me again. Virginia was gone, and there was nothing left keeping me there.

Chapter 20

I MADE THE move to St. Louis, Missouri in early June of 2014. I settled in the Country Club Hills community close to the town of Ferguson. I
moved all my things into the apartment and began to get to know the city. I
explored famous and locally known treasures alike. I visited the Missouri
Botanical Garden, with its 75 acres of green space and plant displays. I
loved the rainforest exhibit; it reminded me of the Sierra Leone of my
youth. I discovered the Lumière Casino and Hotel, a relatively new addition
to the downtown St. Louis area. I had become quite familiar with the fun of
slot machines and card tables at the casino on the LCO reservation.

My greatest culinary find was a local pizzeria, Imo's, which reminded
me of the authentic Italian pizza I grew to love when living in Gioia Tauro,
Italy. In St. Louis the Provel cheese blend used by Imo's is in such great
demand that it's packaged and sold in local grocery stores. The pizza features a cracker thin crust along with the rich marinara sauce and Provel
cheese blend, and is served in squares, hence their slogan "the square beyond compare." I guess my years in Italy made an indelible impression on
my taste buds.

I soon discovered that St. Louis was a diverse community. In fact
Ferguson, in particular, is quite diverse when compared to Milwaukee,
which is one of the most segregated communities in America. Although my
new neighborhood was predominately black, more than 65%, White,
Hispanic, and Asian families lived there, too. I met people from all over the
globe in the grocery stores, gas stations, and churches I began to frequent.

The diversity in Ferguson reminded me of my first summer in Greece where I met migrant workers from so many places. I received numerous invitations to attend places of worship. I felt that at this particular juncture of my life I needed a place of worship and communion, so I kept an open mind and a watchful eye when visiting local churches. I'd attended Catholic mass as a child as part of school. After visiting the Blessed Teresa of Calcutta Catholic parish in Ferguson, I decided now was the time to finally join the Catholic Church. I chose this parish because of the diversity among its members. I looked forward to worshipping with other international citizens. Mass at Blessed Teresa of Calcutta was just as I remembered it from childhood. I listened, prayed and sang and it reminded me of happy times at the missionary school in my village of Punduru.

Frequently the parishioners gather in the basement of the church before or after mass to converse and eat. The convivial spirit and atmosphere is so inviting. I still recall my first pancake breakfast at the church. I was eager to make new friends and looked forward to chatting with the parishioners. Much to my delight I was well received at the breakfast, and everyone I met seemed as eager to make my acquaintance as I was to get to know them.

The parish pastor Reverend Father Robert Rosebrough took a special interest in me and began to get to know me. I told Fr. Rosebrough about myself, my Catholic schooling and special relationships with the School Sisters of Notre Dame from Saint Louis, Missouri. We discussed the nuns' mission and the difference the nuns were able to make in Sierra Leone. After talking with Fr. Rosebrough I made arrangements to complete the Rite of Christian Initiation for Adults (RCIA) as a condition for my membership in the church. The classes met prior to mass for about sixteen weeks and were an opportunity for new members, most of them neighbors, to get to know one another.

The RCIA class started me to thinking more about the various aspects of my life, my relationship to God and especially how I see myself. I resolved that I am a servant of God, so with that in mind I decided to set some goals for myself.

As soon as I joined the church I reached out to Sister Rosanne and the other SSND nuns to update them. I was delighted to discover that some of the nuns were living in South St. Louis, not far from the Botanical Garden. Though we'd kept in touch, I had not laid eyes on the sisters since 1976. Viewing St. Louis as the meeting grounds where I reconnected with someone I'd known for more than 35 years went a long made me feel like I was creating a personal history in St. Louis.

Starting over again, I decided to set some goals for myself. I needed to protect what was left of my self-respect. I was happy about reconnecting with family and decided that nourishing those relationships would be a priority. I also set out on a quest to forgive every person who had ever done anything wrong to me, including myself. I carried an inordinate amount of guilt and regret: guilt over leaving my family and not being home at the time of my mother's death; guilt over missing Tom's funeral; regret over my failed marriage. I regretted ever falling in love with Jessica and cashing those money orders. I felt guilt and regret over not choosing to continue the fight when I felt like my attorney threw me under the bus during the settlement of my second civil rights lawsuit. I harbored anger at myself and the system of things, and I did not like the way it made me feel. Forgiving myself and others was the best way to release my anger and restore peace in my world so that I could once again rebuild my self-worth.

I seized the opportunity to seek forgiveness from Sister Rosanne. During my days in Yengema she had looked out for me and handled my school business with compassion and efficiency. As a boy, I took advantage of her compassion on more than one occasion, and I felt great shame about that. Luckily, the nuns arranged a reunion for me at the Provincial House in South Saint Louis. I felt compelled to reflect on my history and seek out human connection. On the day of the reception, I was filled with the joy of a child on Christmas morning. We had more than 35 years of shared history, and they had known me when I was young. They could attest to my growth over time.

I went to the convent on a boiling hot day in July. At the reunion reception, I was flanked by Sisters Rosanne, Andre, Josephine, Kathy, Eleanor, and Antoinette, all of whom had been at Yengema Secondary School. I was completely overwhelmed with joy and felt blessed as I sat among these nuns who had devoted their entire lives to giving a first class education to children in places that need it most, like Sierra Leone.

Sister Kathy explained that she and another nun had been in Yengema during the horrific and brutal rebel war. I was saddened, disgusted and ashamed when she explained that the rebels had attacked the mother compound at Yengema. My jaw dropped as Sister Kathy described how she was held at gunpoint but still had the presence of mind to confront the rebels and negotiate their release.

Tears stood in my eyes as I listened to her story. I thought about a news report I'd heard about Catholic nuns from America who were murdered during Central American rebel wars. It was all too close. We could have lost them in the blink of an eye. I apologized for my country to the nuns. All present knew that it had been a senseless war fueled by poverty and discontent among the people who'd been exploited over the years.

As the room broke into a half a dozen side conversations, I turned to Sister Rosanne and told her that I always appreciated her care and concern. She looked at me for a long moment and said, "Out with it, Francis. Just like when you were a scrawny little teenager I can still tell when something is on your mind. Tell me please."

I cleared my throat and began, "Please understand. I was bullied in school. Kobe and Arthur and the others tormented me constantly." Sister Rosanne raised an eyebrow and leaned forward without speaking. I sensed that she was waiting for me to continue. I went on, "I lied to you, Sister. The boys all thought that I had money because I was supported by Tom. When it came time for the holiday they knew everyone was going home. They would come to me and say, 'Give us the money. We know you have it.' Every time I tried to explain that Tom did not give me any money directly, they called me a liar and beat me. So, I would come to you and ask for money to take the taxi truck to my village. I always told you a little more than I needed so that I would have cash to pay off the bullies. I know there is no excuse for my behavior, but you have to understand they would hurt me ..." A wide smile spread across Sister Rosanne's face. She took a deep breath and exhaled, "I forgive you, Francis." I felt the weight of the lie lift from my heart. I had never imagined that such simple words could make such a profound difference to my spirit. Sitting beside us, Sister Josephine, who had been my religious teacher, nodded her head in agreement that I had been bullied because I was supported by my friend Thomas Johnson.

Asking her to forgive my lie had revealed to me the necessity of my telling the lie, thereby alleviating my guilt. I did the best I could at the time and had carried a stone in my heart ever since. God had removed the stone from my heart by forgiving my trespasses. It wasn't until after this meeting with Sister Rosanne that I gained a genuine appreciation of the value of forgiving myself.

I left Sister Rosanne that day with a new perspective on forgiveness. After my reunion with the nuns, I got down on my knees and thanked God for giving Sister Kathy the speaking power that convinced the rebels to spare their lives. I thanked God for freeing my heart from the bondage of guilt. I prayed that these lessons would permeate my life.

I was still in the honeymoon phase of getting to know the city and my neighborhood. The streets were clean and the subdivision was usually quiet. Without warning, a series of race riots broke out in the wake of the shooting death of unarmed, 18-year-old Michael Brown, Jr. by Ferguson police officer Darren Wilson. On a hot day in August, I was leaving Schnucks grocery store in the West Florissant Avenue shopping center when I saw scores of police cruisers speeding north with their sirens blazing. What could be so serious? I wondered. I purposely drove in the opposite direction of all the police cars, taking the long way home. I guess I imagined there had been a bad car wreck.

That night on the news I sat speechless as I watched the report of how Michael Brown lay dead in the street for hours. I thought how awful for his family. Why didn't the police move the body? The community immediately began to mourn the loss of one of its youth. Neighbors demanded the arrest of the 28-year-old white police officer. News reports began to reveal a trend of discriminatory practices throughout the law enforcement system in Ferguson, MO, and neighbors insisted that the shooting was racially motivated.

The days and weeks following the shooting saw riot behavior, and several homes and businesses were torched and burned to the ground. I couldn't help but think of the rebels in Sierra Leone. What gave these people the right to destroy other people's property? The news reported that vandals from other parts of the city were invading the small suburban community, looting local businesses and disturbing the peace. The intersection of West

Florissant and South Florissant in front of the municipal and police buildings in downtown Ferguson became the epicenter of protests and demonstrations. The whole area became the scene of national and international news reports.

I was afraid for my personal safety and the security of my home. There were often protestor blocking the road, and a curfew was instituted. Sirens could be heard all throughout the night. I had never seen anything like it. The image in the media of black protestors and white police in riot gear set opposite one another could have been taken in the 1960s. How could this be happening in modern America, 50 years later? My own unfortunate encounter with the American judicial system had already irreparably altered my American dream, and even still I was shocked by what I saw. This shouldn't be happening in the most advanced nation of the world.

I still felt myself a stranger in my new city. I resolved to keep my head down and focus on my job search. Every time I watched the news it reopened the wound. I sympathized with the anger of the people against local law enforcement and the white establishment in general. But I was afraid of where all the anger and violence would lead. I didn't want to find myself living in ruins right here on American soil. Needless to say it was difficult to keep forgiveness as a goal when there was so much negativity and anger flying around.

News reports detailing the racism and coercion behind all the events surrounding Michael Brown's death struck an especially sour chord with me. I had wanted to believe that the racism I experienced in Hayward and Milwaukee were due to the predominately white social structure of those places—the bureaucratic machinery of the State of Wisconsin in particular. The idea that a large, almost 50% black, metropolitan area like St. Louis could also harbor racial prejudice among its law enforcement was more than a little disturbing. I wondered how all of this would be resolved.

In the wake of the shooting death of Mike Brown, Jr. I found my church congregation somber and remorseful. I noticed my neighbors were withdrawn and appeared tired in the mist of all the racial tensions and publicity. In spite of the unrest, frustration and negativity, I noticed the spirit of my fellow parishioners appeared alive, and each Sunday we congregated at mass and prayed together. I was quite delighted when the Archbishop of

Saint Louis, the Most Reverend Robert Carlson, visited our parish in his efforts to facilitate healing and reconciliation. My church often recited a special prayer for the Brown family for justice to be done. Throughout the ordeal Father Rosebrough held the congregation together in prayer, faith and spirit and on several occasions Father Rosebrough joined other clergy in downtown Ferguson and led prayer vigils for healing and reconciliation in the community.

In the height of the unrest and frustration in the community, Fr. Rosebrough invited me and several other black parishioners to have dinner with him at his residence. I sensed the mood among my fellow black parishioners was mixed. On one hand, there was a feeling of remorsefulness and exhaustion from all the racial negativity and national press publicity. On the other hand, I truly felt and sensed the spirit and faith of my fellow black parishioners come alive as we dined and prayed with Fr. Rosebrough for God's healing mercy, grace, and conciliation in the community.

I noticed Fr. Rosebrough listened attentively to my fellow parishioners as they expressed their feelings and opinions on the ongoing unrest in the community. I must admit I felt a genuine sympathy for Fr. Rosebrough as he continued to minister to our diverse faith community. It was during our dinner with Fr. Rosebrough that he disclosed he has decided to commission the portraits of the Reverend Father Augustus Tolton and Sister Thea Bowman to be hung on the walls inside our parish. Father Tolton was born a slave in Missouri in 1854 and became the first black Roman Catholic minister in the United States (ordained in 1886). Sister Bowman was a granddaughter of a slave from Mississippi who joined the Catholic Church and became nun. Fr. Rosebrough told us that he thought the new devotionals would be a great opportunity to educate the congregation on the full history of the church. Fr. Tolton and Sr. Bowman both clearly demonstrate diversity in the history of the Catholic Church. I was impressed at how thoughtful the church's administration was. The visibility of the portraits of the black clergy members displayed in the church added character and increased my feelings of being at home at Blessed Teresa's in Ferguson, Missouri.

A few months after the shooting I heard news reports of prosecutorial misconduct that may have played a significant role in influencing the grand jury not to indict the Officer Darren Wilson. There were also news reports and published grand jury testimony that stated Mike Brown reached through Officer Wilson's cruiser's window and reached for the officer's gun. I did not know what to make of this turn of events. I continued to be unsettled by the unrest in the community. I was overwhelmed with disgust at news reports of prosecutorial misconduct in the case. I was reminded of the Sawyer County prosecutor's misconduct in my case in 2005. I knew how it felt to stand in front of the business end of an angry prosecutor's weapon. While I reserved my personal judgment about the role the St. Louis County prosecutor may have played in the Michael Brown case, in light of the wide discretions prosecutors have to determine whether or not to charge and the latitude prosecutors are given to predict and determine the outcomes of cases, I was at least suspicious of the circumstances surrounding the alleged misinformation given to the grand jury. I prayed, *God, how could one so young be taken so early? Touch now all who would oppose your will. Speak justice and it will be.*

I had to pull my attention away from the television news, because it depressed me and became a barrier to my development of a healthy mental state. I turned my focus to my job search, scouring the Internet for openings in the corrections field, as well as related jobs. I submitted dozens of applications. I checked my mailbox and my email constantly. At first I was engulfed by the tasks of preparing resumes and cover letters, but after a while I became anxious about the lack of response I was getting to my applications. My worst fear was that my wrongful criminal prosecution and my civil rights lawsuits against the State of Wisconsin might render me unemployable.

I also knew that Internet search engines were among the first avenues employers use when they begin background checks on potential hires. I Googled myself and almost fell out of my chair; I must admit that I had a mini-meltdown when I read the screen. There was no denying it: the Internet search engines were populated with public information, including news reports of my wrongful prosecution as well as the federal court decisions, orders and reports of my civil rights lawsuits against the State of Wisconsin. When my heart stopped racing, I resolved to accept the reality that the information was out there. I reasoned that I could easily explain these things in an interview if given the chance.

I remained hopeful and determined; after all, I had always been a survivor. I vowed not to give up looking for work, and I began to objectively evaluate my chances of ever finding a job again in the field of corrections, or any related corrections employment given my record on the Internet. Would I ever find an employer willing to hire me, or even give me the opportunity to explain my public record? What employer would want to risk hiring a guy who had successfully sued his former employer twice? I expanded my job search to explore other parallel positions.

The St. Louis County Family Court advertised several entry level positions. I reasoned that I had 14 years of experience as Senior Probation and Parole Agent, which made me more than qualified for the position of Deputy Juvenile Probation Officer. Alas, I was rejected. I also applied to numerous private and nonprofit agencies with corrections-related vacancies, with the same result.

I stumbled upon a contractual job vacancy for the position of Correctional Counselor I at the Southwestern Illinois Correctional Center in East St. Louis, a minimum security prison that provides drug and alcohol treatment services with the State of Illinois, Department of Corrections. I submitted my job materials and was delighted when I was offered the position of Counselor I. Time to break out the champagne.

Much to my dismay, the State of Illinois Department of Corrections notified me that I was prohibited from providing services to the Illinois DOC because of my criminal record involving forgery of US Postal money orders. The news let the air out of my balloon. I prayed, *Lord I am doing everything required of me. Why isn't it working? I pray that if this job is for me you make a way for me like you have done so many times before. In Jesus' precious and holy name I pray.*

I called the DOC and asked if there was any way I could speak to the person who made the decision to deny my employment. The representative explained an appeal process, of which I immediately took advantage. I provided the administrative review board a detailed explanation of the unwarranted charges and wrongful prosecution in Wisconsin, in addition to the investigative findings showing that the prosecutor was reprimanded for her actions. I also provided a letter written on my behalf by my defense attorney. I submitted my materials and resolved to wait. Before long a decision came down in my favor. I concluded that God had, indeed, made a way for me yet again.

By the start of spring I felt myself firmly established in my new home town. Sisters Rosanne and Josephine both attended my Rite of Initiation at the Easter Vigil ceremony that was held in the parish during which I received the sacraments of baptism and confirmation. Sister Rosanne spoke to the whole church about her mission in Africa. Her words were both joyful and hopeful. She shared with all present that she'd been my mentor at Yengema Secondary School and that we'd stayed in contact since 1976. I felt proud to be associated with this woman who was a missionary, educator and a faithful servant of God. This event was yet another milestone in my establishing a personal history in St. Louis.

I continue to work on forgiveness, and struggle with regret from the past. My own life story has shown me that hope is the most powerful weapon that we can arm ourselves with. I continue to believe and trust in God, knowing that through Christ all things are possible and there are always bright spots waiting to be discovered.

An added bonus to my job is my trek to work. Nothing compares to the scenic view beside the lakes and in the forests of Hayward, Wisconsin, but my daily drive over the Mississippi River is a close second. The muddy Mississippi is far from fit to swim or fish in, but still it reminds me of the River Sewa in Sierra Leone. Crossing the Mississippi River every day as I drive to work makes me feel like I'm getting a tour of history. These two powerful and important bodies of water mark the passing of time in my life. As a boy I watched the Sewa rise and fall with the seasons, and now as a man I watch the same pattern over the Mississippi. But there are no diamonds in Missouri, so I imagine what the barges carry from day to day. My morning commutes are always a nice mix of nostalgia and contemplation. I arrive to work with a well of gratitude.

In spite of it all, I still believe in the equality, liberty, and fraternity that the Statute of Liberty represents. In my American dream I am able to stand on my own two feet and earn a living without being troubled by past prejudice. I dream that America will revisit its founding principles and obliterate poverty, racism, and injustice.

Racial prejudice has always been a difficult topic for me. On several occasions I've withdrawn from conversations that devolved into white bashing. Having known and experienced the affections and care of a man like Tom means that I can never make a general negative statement based on whiteness. Tom didn't choose me without consideration for my race, but rather I think he chose me because of it. Tom recognized that God had situated him to be a blessing in the life of another, and I was that other. Tom chose a boy: poor, black, and in need of education. Without Tom my prospects for the future would have been bleak. His gift gave me hope, and his friendship gave me the strength to learn, explore and strike out on my own.

My story has more than a "great white hope" plot. I loved and respected Tom because he was a servant of God who happened to be white, just as I feel I am a servant of God who happens to be black and from Africa. My story is about how God saves, God provides, and God heals. Every day we are given opportunities to love our fellow man, opportunities to see past the surface of our beings, opportunities to help in big and small ways. It was a white man who taught me that we should never waste those opportunities, and instead get involved.

God has used many of his servants to bless and comfort me over the years. Tom's help made it possible for me to establish a meaningful life in the United States. The friendly encounters I have had with people around the globe far outweigh the terrible acts of racism and bullying I have experienced at the hands of both black and white people. I have worked to forgive the bad acts of the cruel ones, and in the interim I renew my commitment to living a full life according to God's divine plan for my life.

Photo Gallery

My nieces pounding rice behind my sister's mud brick house.

My sisters Bettie and Amie and extended family members.

The forests around Punduru

You are now entering the heart of the diamond zone—National Diamond
Mining Company (SL) Ltd headquartered at Yengema

My beloved Yengema Secondary School

Life at boarding school (front row with wrist watch) year before graduation
in 1979

Not enough room for all these passengers

Crossing the Strait of Messina onboard the Strait of Messina—between
Villa San Giovanni and Messina

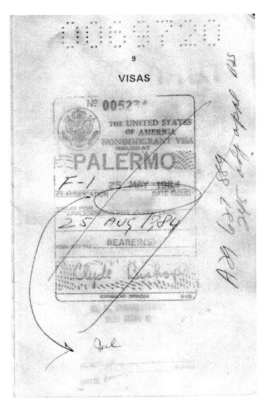

May 25, 1984—day of reckoning for me in Palermo, Sicily

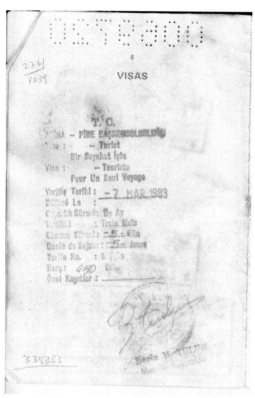

Istanbul, Turkey—where East and West travelers use to meet.

I miss the Greece I knew in 1983

As a British subject, I was proud to walk the streets of London

About the Author

Francis Mandewah received his Masters degree in Public Administration from American International College in Springfield, Massachusetts, in 1991. A social justice advocate, he has 14 years experience as a probation and parole agent with the Wisconsin Department of Corrections. He is a member of Blessed Teresa of Calcutta Parish in Ferguson, Missouri, where he currently resides and works as a counselor at a correctional facility.

CPSIA information can be obtained
at www.ICGtesting.com
Printed in the USA
FFOW02n1802230516
24357FF